THIRTEEN LOOPS

B. J. HOLLARS

THE UNIVERSITY OF ALABAMA PRESS • TUSCALOOSA

RACE, VIOLENCE, AND THE LAST LYNCHING IN AMERICA

THIRTEEN
LOOPS

The University of Alabama Press
Tuscaloosa, Alabama 35487-0380
All rights reserved
Manufactured in the United States of America

Typeface: Minion Pro and Gill Sans
Design by Michele Myatt Quinn

∞

Cover photo: United Klans of America Rally, Mobile, Alabama,
1977. Photo by Dave Hamby, courtesy of the *Mobile Press-Register.*

The paper on which this book is printed meets the minimum
requirements of American National Standard for Information
Sciences—Permanence of Paper for Printed Library Materials,
ANSI Z39.48-1984.

Library of Congress Cataloging-in-Publication Data

Hollars, B. J.
    Thirteen loops : race, violence, and the last lynching in America
/ B.J. Hollars.
        p. cm.
    Includes bibliographical references and index.
    ISBN 978-0-8173-1753-9 (cloth : alk. paper) — ISBN 978-0-
8173-8582-8 (electronic) 1. Lynching—Alabama—History—20th
century. 2. Violence—Alabama—History—20th century. 3. Racism—
Alabama—History—20th century. 4. Alabama—Race relations—
History—20th century. 5. Mobile (Ala.)—Race relations—History—
20th century. 6. Birmingham (Ala.)—Race relations—History—
20th century. 7. Tuscaloosa (Ala.)—Race relations—History—20th
century. 8. Donald, Michael, 1961–1981. 9. Maddox, Vaudine, d.
1933. 10. Ballard, Gene, d. 1979. I. Title.
    HV6465.A2H65 2011
    364.1′34–dc22

                                              2011003388

To the victims, of whom there are many.

CONTENTS

PART III Untangling

ACKNOWLEDGMENTS

This book would not have been possible without the incredible efforts of various journalists, archivists, interviewees, and advisors.

Thank you to the wonderful reporting set forth in the *Tuscaloosa News,* the *Birmingham News,* and the *Mobile Register.* Kathy Jumper's and Michael Wilson's reporting, in particular, proved invaluable.

Scotty Kirkland of the University of South Alabama Archives managed the insurmountable task of putting together the Michael Donald Collection and was gracious enough to share his work with me.

Thank you to Morris Dees, Steve Fiffer, and their book *A Season for Justice,* which offers a unique view inside the civil trial.

The Southern Poverty Law Center was also kind enough to open its doors to me, for which I am grateful.

Similarly, I am grateful for having had the opportunity to speak to so many thoughtful and considerate people: Star Bloom, Richard Cohen, Bob Eddy, Glenn Feldman, Chris Galanos, Kalliopi Hartley, Richard Kerger, Dr. LeRoy Riddick, Kathy Sutton, Penny Weaver, and Police Chief Wilbur Williams.

Thanks to Joshua Weinberg of the Discovery Channel for allowing me use of the phrase "The Last Lynching."

To Dan Waterman at The University of Alabama Press.

To Drs. Wendy Rawlings, Stephen Schneider, and Lisa Lindquist Dorr.

And of course, to Michael Martone, whose guidance in this endeavor helped keep the train on the tracks.

To my family, who have believed in my words since the first one.

And finally, to my wife, who allowed me to dedicate my days and nights to conjuring the ever-present ghosts of history.

THIRTEEN LOOPS

INTRODUCTION
Braiding the Rope

The hangman's knot is not a difficult knot to learn.

First, make a U-shaped bight, then a second bight, then an N-shape. Next, take the working end around the bight until it turns back in on itself. Work away from the noose, wrapping the desired number of loops around the coil.

Pull down.

Tighten.

Constrict.

This information is readily available on *Wikipedia*, along with a helpful illustration.

"Each additional coil adds friction to the knot, which makes the noose harder to pull closed or open," the website explains. "The number of coils should therefore be adjusted depending on the intended use, the type and thickness of rope, and environmental conditions such as wet or greasy rope. Six to eight loops are normal when using natural ropes. One coil makes it equivalent to the simple slipknot."

If I know how to tie a simple slipknot, do I know how to tie a noose?

There were thirteen loops on the hangman's knot around Michael Donald's neck.

According to *Wikipedia*, it must have been a difficult knot to pull open.

People are hanged for any number of reasons.

They are hanged for arson, they are hanged for robbery, they are hanged for suspected robbery. They are hanged for assault, for attempted assault, for incendiarism, for suspicion of rape, for attempted rape, for alleged rape, for rape, for burglary, for wife beating, for suspected murder, for attempted murder, for alleged murder, for alleged complicity in murder, for murder, for barn burning, for alleged barn burning, for self-defense, for poisoning mules, for poisoning wells, for alleged well poisoning, for insulting whites, for debt, for no offense, or for being black, among various other offenses.

In 1893, Alabama registered the most hangings for the year at twenty-five, followed by twenty-four in Georgia, eighteen in Louisiana, seventeen in Mississippi, fifteen in South Carolina, ten in Tennessee, ten in Virginia, eight in Texas, eight in Kentucky, seven in Arkansas, seven in Florida, three in Missouri, two in Kansas, three in Illinois, one in New York, and one in Indian Territory. Yet the total of one hundred and fifty-nine reported lynching victims of 1893 was dramatically dwarfed by the two hundred and forty-one from the previous year.

Listed beneath their crime, journalist Ida B. Wells recorded their names, as well as the date of their hanging and the city in which they were hanged.

Benjamin Jackson of Jackson, Mississippi, was an alleged well poisoner, so he was hanged on September 15, 1893.

Charles Martin of Shelby County, Tennessee, was charged with no offense, so he was hanged on July twenty-first of that year.

On Christmas Day, Calvin Thomas was hanged near Bainbridge, Georgia, for assault.

A month prior, on November 4, Edward Wagner, William Wagner, Samuel Motlow, and Eliza Motlow allegedly burned a barn, so they were hanged in Lynchburg, Virginia, comprising 40 percent of the total number of people officially hanged in the state that year.

Sometimes the sheer number of names makes it easy to forget that once these were real people.

But they were.

The Wagners and the Motlows were real people.

And then they were hanged.

Allegedly, they'd burned a barn.

In 1930, on a cool summer night in Marion, Indiana, Tom Shipp and Abe Smith were hanged for allegedly raping a young white woman and murdering the man she was with.

A third person—sixteen-year-old James Cameron—was accused of the same crime.

But as the throngs of people began tightening the noose around his neck, they were interrupted. A man—believed to be either the raped girl's uncle or the head of the local American Legion—stood atop a car, informing the mob of Cameron's innocence. Others report the man was actually Marion Police Captain Charles Truex, who lied to the crowd in an attempt to save Cameron's life, claiming the young black boy had only been arrested for stealing chickens. Regardless of his identity, the man said stop so they stopped, allowing the rope to hang limp.

Later, it was reported that a woman's voice had actually called through the crowd, halting the murder, though James Cameron complicated the matter by claiming that it had not been a mortal voice, but rather, belonged to the Virgin Mary.

Stranger still, those directly involved in the mob didn't recall hearing a voice at all.

Our Town author Cynthia Carr notes the frustration of trying to corroborate the details of the Marion lynching, explaining, "Nailing down the simplest facts about this event was never simple."

She admits that there were too many versions of the truth, too many "conflicting narratives and endless unknowables."

Later that evening, when the police arrived in Marion from neighboring towns, they reported "a scene of peace and remarkable good humor." Writer James H. Madison recounts, "One of the mob who had helped with the rope went with his young wife to a nearby restaurant for a late dinner . . . A woman nursed her baby. Fathers held up older children to see the two bodies. Many stood on top of cars."

Time magazine quotes Prosecuting Attorney Harley Hardin as noting that, "The self-satisfaction of the people over the lynching is a psychological matter resting on dissatisfaction with verdicts returned by juries and the sentences imposed. The people feel that the only way to get justice is to take the law into their own hands"—a rationale that would be utilized far into the future.

That night, Cameron suffered little more than a rope burn while the other men dangled from trees.

Perhaps you've seen a picture.

Or a postcard.

Tom Shipp and Abe Smith became famous.

Soon after the lynching, a Jewish schoolteacher from New York named Abel Meeropol stumbled across a photo of the Marion murders and was inspired to write the infamous lyrics to Billie Holiday's antilynching song, "Strange Fruit."

Meeropol later became known as the adoptive father of Julius and Ethel Rosenberg's children, though he is still remembered most for his poignant lyrics. Yet while his metaphorical interpretation of the brutal crime became the anthem of the antilynching movement, his poetic rendering of a horrific lynching does little to help us better understand the definition of the term itself.

According to the *Oxford English Dictionary,* the term "lynch" means, "To condemn and punish by lynch law. In early use, implying chiefly the infliction of punishment such as whipping, tarring and feathering, or the like; now only, to inflict sentence of death by lynch law."

In his 1933 seminal work, *Lynching and the Law,* James Harmon Chadbourn framed it differently, defining it as "a protest against the inefficiency of courts as agencies for the punishment of crime," as well as a physical expression "of distrust in the efficacy of legal processes in the given case."

In 1995, Glenn Feldman updated the definition yet again, calling lynching a "public, summary judgment handed down by a community allied in sympathies and prejudices."

These varied definitions lead one to believe that the complications involved in defining the term speak directly to the inexplicable nature of the crimes to which the word is attributed. Yet Christopher Waldrep drew another conclusion, noting, "The different meanings of the word over time indicate that antilynching reformers understood discourse as central to their struggle and fought hard to control it." Waldrep argues that the word was a tool, and that the debate on its meaning evolved as a result of various antilynching groups' struggling to decide how best to harness the word's power.

The antilynching movement of the twentieth century became a battle between quantitative and qualitative analysis, Waldrep citing Ida B. Wells and W.E.B. Du Bois as two examples of reformers who relied on statistics to drive their case. Du Bois's training as a social scientist led him to believe that racism might be toppled by numerical values; that facts, figures, and raw data on racial crimes might serve as an entry point for rational thought. However, in April 1899, upon learning of the brutal lynching of Sam Hose—how according to Waldrep, the white perpetrators "displayed the dead man's knuckles in an Atlanta grocery store"—Du Bois began to second-guess his approach. "In the face of such shocking barbarity," Waldrep writes, "science hardly seemed enough . . . Instead of relying on spare facts, Du Bois invoked rhetoric to persuade."

While the definition continued to evolve, this evolution did not always translate to an improved clarity. Yet both past and present scholars agree that to lynch someone does not necessarily mean to hang a person from a tree by a noose. Instead, it simply implies a brand of vigilante justice in which citizens punish the accused prior to a legal trial. While hanging is typically associated with the term, it is not a necessary component.

Joel Williamson, author of *A Rage for Order,* extends the definition far beyond violent means, noting the term's "sophisticated variations." He writes: "One could lynch just as effectively by genteel means as crudely by rope and faggot. Negroes could be lynched by account books. And they could be lynched by written history. They could be blamed retroactively for the Civil War and for the alleged excesses of Reconstruction." The definition of "lynch" manages to encompass all of this, greatly expanding beyond the prototypical views of bodies swinging from trees.

In recent history, perhaps the most memorable use of the word was offered by Supreme Court Justice Clarence Thomas during his Senate confirmation hearings in October 1991, in which he claimed that the sexual harassment allegation brought against him was an example of a "high-tech lynching"—a phrase which many considered a debasement of the term. Thomas claimed that unless powerful blacks were willing to "kowtow to an old order," they would be "lynched, destroyed, caricatured by a committee of the U.S. Senate rather than hung from a tree."

With Thomas's spirited response, the word returned to the American consciousness, assuming it ever left.

❖

In order to claim Michael Donald's 1981 murder "the last lynching in America," we must first examine subsequent acts that also fall into this category. It's difficult to differentiate between a lynching and a hate crime, and when we look to one example—the murder of Matthew Shepard, which occurred on October 12, 1998, near Laramie, Wyoming—we begin to question why the media and the court system framed it with one term rather than another. After all, Shepard—a twenty-one-year-old Caucasian killed as a result of his sexuality—seems to fit neatly within the boundaries of Chadbourn, Feldman, Waldrep, and Williamson's various definitions. Yet perhaps the word "lynching" seemed too archaic for a country on the cusp of the twenty-first century, whereas the phrase "hate crime" (much like the word "lynching" in the early twentieth century) better served as a versatile, legislative tool.

While the Civil Rights Act of 1968 would eventually help pave the way for hate crime legislation, the phrase itself would become popularized as a result of various legislative efforts proposed and passed from the late 1980s to the present, such as the Hate Crimes Statistic Act of 1990, the Campus Hate Crimes Right to Know Act of 1997, and most recently, the Hate Crimes Prevention Act signed into law in October 2009. Though scholars and lawmakers have yet to settle on an all-encompassing definition for "hate crime," several possibilities have been set forth. Nathan Hall's *Hate Crime* grapples with this lack of semantic uniformity, though for the purposes herein, we will rely upon the U.S. Hate Crimes Statistic Act definition that Hall reports as "Crimes that manifest evidence of prejudice based on race, religion, sexual orientation or ethnicity."

While the crimes wrought against Michael Donald and Matthew Shepard both qualify as hate crimes under this definition, the terminology seems to have evolved somewhere between Donald's death in 1981 and Shepard's seventeen years later.

The racially motivated murder of forty-nine-year-old African-American James Byrd Jr. may also have contributed to this shift in terminology. In June 1998, just months before Shepard's death, Byrd was chained to the back of a pickup truck and dragged three miles down a country road in Jasper, Texas, while three white men leered from inside the truck's cab. The men were later convicted of murder, and two of them were sentenced to death row while the third received life in prison. While this case, much like Matthew Shepard's, qualifies within the definition of "lynching," it involved none of the historical lynching tools—no trees, no ropes, no nooses.

The term "mob" is equally convoluted. While the *Oxford English Dictionary*'s definition—"to attack or surround in"—appears quite self-explanatory, it still leaves various questions unanswered.

Such as: How many people constitute a mob?

The 1922 Dyer Anti-Lynching Bill brought before Congress finally put the question to rest. The legislation defined a mob as "an assemblage composed of three or more persons acting in concert for the purpose of depriving any person of his life without authority of law as a punishment for or to prevent the commission of some actual or supposed public offense."

Yet how do we account for the arbitrariness of defining a mob as three? And does the 1922 definition still hold firm so many years after the fact? Why not four or five? Why not a dozen? And what are we to call it if two men act instead, as was the case on a Mobile night in 1981. Years after Michael Donald's death—after I saw a photo of him hanging there in his Converse tennis shoes—I couldn't help asking myself: Is the number not irrelevant when the outcome remains the same?

This is the story of the interconnectedness of three innocent victims, all of whom suffered violent deaths through no fault of their own:

Vaudine Maddox (1933, Tuscaloosa), Sergeant Gene Ballard (1979, Birmingham), and Michael Donald (1981, Mobile). While the death of Vaudine Maddox is not directly tied to the deaths of Sergeant Ballard or Michael Donald, it serves as a cautionary tale that illuminates the cultural fears and biases of the time period. It is also a premonition of the violence that would occur in the same region nearly fifty years later. Likewise, Maddox's murder—as well as the murders of the accused (though never convicted) African-American perpetrators—functions as a lens to support the historical framework of lynching. I have imposed this link to add a much-needed backdrop for the other victims. While it is true that almost any historical case might have achieved the same end, Tuscaloosa's racial violence best depicts a Southern town set ablaze—a theme that reemerges in Mobile in 1981. Further, the Tuscaloosa story offers an example of racial murders that found no justice, presenting a clear juxtaposition to the Donald murder in which justice was finally served.

However, the deaths of Sergeant Gene Ballard and Michael Donald *are* inextricably linked, two threads woven together by circumstances beyond their control. The two never met—had no knowledge of one another's existence—yet their connectedness would forever alter the fabric of United States' race relations. This book sets out to trace their transference, examining the light they cast upon one another and the shadows cast upon them.

Parsing fact from fiction was no simple task, and I initially found myself examining ancient newspapers in an attempt to stumble across something worth believing. I never expected to tackle such a subject, nor did I feel qualified to do so. But as I continued researching, I became invested in recounting the stories the victims themselves could no longer tell. It is my great hope that this perspective of relating three separate murders might offer a fresh lens through which to view the oft-trodden terrain of Southern racial violence without resorting to sensationalism or hyperbole.

In matters such as these, the truth is often enough.

While this book examines the deaths of Vaudine Maddox, Sergeant Gene Ballard, and Michael Donald, Donald remains the focus. My attempts at understanding his story, in particular, led me deep into Alabama, requiring me to ask difficult questions while dialing numbers and sending letters to strangers.

However, throughout the course of this project, I was continually astounded by people's willingness to assist in uncovering the truth. The deeper I delved, the more I relied upon people I'd never met, perfect strangers willing to help.

Yet that is not always the case.

Thirty years ago—on the night of March 20, 1981—two strangers pulled to the side of a Mobile street and called nineteen-year-old Michael Donald over to their car.

They asked him for directions to a nightclub.

They asked him to come closer.

Throughout this project, I followed him as far as I could.

PART I   Tying the Knot

FIRST LOOP
A PAIL OF FLOUR

Tuscaloosa, June–August 1933

I asked the Lord to bring me back to Tuscaloosa.

Vaudine Maddox walked with a pail of flour. The early morning sun crept through the trees as the twenty-one-year-old white girl shuffled along the clay road in Big Sandy, twelve miles outside of Tuscaloosa. Situated an hour south of Birmingham and on the border of the Alabama Black Belt, 1930s Tuscaloosa, as described by author Philip Beidler, was a "sleepy, middle-sized city distinguished mainly by the dual presences of the state university and the state hospital for the insane." Clarence Cason, a native Alabamian and the head of the university's journalism department from 1928 to 1935, noted the city's "serene and comfortable beauty," calling it the type of place "where one may look forward with happiness to spending the rest of his days." His contemporary, Carl Carmer—a Northerner who accepted a position in the university's English department in 1927—offered a similar assessment, acknowledging Tuscaloosa's "picturesque quality," describing afternoons spent on the golf course and evenings "alive with small impromptu parties." He also noted the town's oppressive heat, how "swimming parties on the Black Warrior River [were] frequent"—a momentary respite for citizens to stave off the swelter.

The weather on Monday, June 12, 1933, was no exception. The day started off cool, though by noon, temperatures reached a stifling ninety-one degrees, sending Alabamians sprawling beneath the shade trees.

Vaudine was the oldest of four siblings. After her mother's death nine years prior, she took charge of the house and began caring for her brothers and sisters, as well as her father and twenty-five-year-old cousin.

All seven shared a run-down, two-room shack on the outskirts of a plantation. Though the Maddox family was white, they were poor, and so lived in a predominantly black community.

Across the woods from her family's shack lived an elderly white couple whom Vaudine assisted with odd jobs, tasks their brittle bodies could no longer perform. As Vaudine and her neighbors discovered, when supplies ran low, it was easier to share from their own reserves than make the dust-filled trip into town.

And so, that morning, Vaudine woke early, slipping into the pantry to fill a pail of flour for her neighbors.

They never received it.

The day after Vaudine's murder, the *Tuscaloosa News* reported, "Tentative theories in the inquiry indicate clearly that someone 'friendly' to the Maddox girl either actually committed the crime or possesses guilty knowledge in connection with it. A small pail of flour which the girl had been carrying to the neighbor's house was found beside a tree trunk at the side of the road."

The sheriff's department concluded that the untouched pail pointed to the possibility that Vaudine had placed it down of her own accord while taking a seat on a log alongside an acquaintance—proof enough for Tuscaloosa Sheriff R. L. Fayette Shamblin that Vaudine knew her murderer.

Monday and Tuesday passed with no sign of Vaudine, though her father didn't appear overly concerned, assuming she'd "just gone off with somebody." But by midafternoon on Wednesday, June 14, Vaudine's younger sisters, Gladys and Audis, proved their father wrong—stumbling across their eldest sister's bloodied body in a ravine a quarter mile from their shack. Vultures circled overhead, small animals gathering around the three-day-old corpse in the woods. The sheriff's department was contacted, though before facts were in place, rumors of a young white girl's rape and murder caused the citizens' blood to boil.

Vaudine's body was taken to the coroner for further study, though the late stages of decomposition made securing additional information difficult. Still, facts began emerging, most importantly, the discovery of the murder weapon: two bloodstained rocks.

The officers crouched over the rocks in the Big Sandy wilderness, shifting the focus of their investigation from *how* she was murdered to *why*.

But Sheriff Shamblin had another question as well: Had Vaudine Maddox been raped prior to her death?

Shamblin anxiously awaited the coroner's results, though after a thorough examination, the coroner offered more questions than answers, citing that the body's three days in the woods made any signs of rape impossible to determine with certainty.

On the morning of the murder, a witness stated that an eighteen-year-old black man named Dan Pippen Jr. was spotted walking past a field near where Vaudine's body was later discovered. A second witness reported that earlier in the day, Pippen had picked up a rock, boasting that he was planning to kill somebody with it.

Neither the police nor the newspapers could confirm these allegations. Nevertheless, despite an alibi from his employer—African-American landowner Will Jemison—Pippen was taken into Sheriff Shamblin's custody by noon on Friday, June 16.

The *Tuscaloosa News* reported that Jemison wasn't alone in having seen Pippen at work during the time of the murder. In Pippen's defense, several fellow employees confirmed his whereabouts on that early Monday morning, and no physical evidence linked him to the murder. Even the newspaper acknowledged the flimsiness of the case, calling it "inconclusive and based principally upon circumstantial evidence."

Sheriff Shamblin ignored the criticism.

"Dan Pippen, Jr., was without court record;" claimed one report, "he had finished the course at the local one-teacher school; he took a very active part in church work, and had sung in a quartette and read a paper at the local church service on the Sunday before the Maddox girl was murdered."

Still, Shamblin remained unmoved.

Regardless of character testimony, a strong alibi, and a dearth of physical evidence, the Tuscaloosa authorities had all the proof they required.

After all, Pippen *did* live within half a mile of the Maddoxes' shack. And further, Pippen and Vaudine were known to have been acquaintances, one report even claiming that they had recently bickered over whether or not to shear a dog. His proximity, in conjunction with his and Vaudine's knowledge of one another's existence, was, in Sheriff Shamblin's eyes, sufficient for the arrest. The unverifiable testimony that he had supposedly threatened to kill someone with a rock seemed only to further solidify the case against him.

Within days of the murder, Shamblin assured Tuscaloosa that he was confident he had successfully apprehended Vaudine Maddox's murderer.

At least he was confident he had one of them.

Two days later, on Sunday, June 18, fifteen-year-old African-American A. T. Harden was taken into sheriff's custody as well. While no physical evidence linked Harden to the crime, either, after a day behind bars, the young black boy was more than willing to confess that he had witnessed Pippen raping and murdering the girl.

Despite his cooperation, Sheriff Shamblin decided to keep Harden in custody as well, at least until the conclusion of the trial.

Finding himself still behind bars after offering the story he believed would exonerate him, Harden quickly retracted his tale. While he initially claimed he and Pippen had crossed paths with Vaudine on the morning of June 12—that Pippen had told him to "stand aside" while he thrust her into the brush and out of view—Harden quickly recanted.

"It's all a lie," he admitted to the sheriff, claiming he'd simply been intimidated by the questioning.

But Shamblin refused to budge. The inconsistencies in Harden's testimony were all the more reason to keep him locked up. Just for good measure, later that day, Sheriff Shamblin also arrested Dan Pippen Jr.'s father for supposedly interfering with his son's investigation.

While there were now two black teenagers and a grown man behind bars in less than a week, the citizens of Tuscaloosa found themselves continually dissatisfied with the slow speed of justice. Two black teens and Pippen Sr. behind bars weren't enough. They required sentencing, and if the courts couldn't find the time to do so, the citizens knew men who could.

On the night of June 21—exactly one week after the discovery of Vaudine's body—a mob of "unattached young men and teen-age boys"

began collecting on Greensboro Avenue. Just before midnight, they gathered at the county jail.

Let's see the prisoners, they demanded. *We want to get a look at 'em.*

Sensing trouble hours before, Sheriff Shamblin agreed to transport Pippen Jr. and Harden to the Birmingham jail just before nightfall. Meanwhile, in Tuscaloosa, the mob continued to grow.

While the mob was informed that Harden and Pippen Jr. were no longer being held in the county jail, Walton Morris and Bernard Marler demanded to see for themselves. The sheriff agreed, and it was only after Walton and Bernard concluded their examination of the county jail and were denied entrance to the city jail that they grudgingly informed the crowd to disperse.

While the *Tuscaloosa News* refused to call it a mob—preferring the term "jail gathering"—it did note that the "gathering" consisted of approximately one hundred onlookers, along with a few dozen cars lining up and down Greensboro. The semantics were important, particularly for a Southern newspaper during this time period.

"It appeared less like a mob than any group I have ever seen gathered for a similar occasion," remarked Judge Henry Foster. "It was not an inflamed spirit and was easily and peacefully dispersed after the curiosity of the boys had been satisfied."

Less than a week later, three young men, including Walton Morris (a Tuscaloosa High football player) and Bernard Marler ("a former star halfback" according to the *Tuscaloosa News*) were arrested and required to pay $1,500 bonds for conspiracy to commit a felony and unlawful assembly, a steep fine for simply gathering around a jail as had been reported.

Yet on the night of the first mob, not a single person was arrested. The judge's tempered words cooled the high tensions and encouraged the young men to return home, seemingly satisfied.

As the days wore on, their satisfaction wouldn't last.

❖

The summer sweltered on, tensions as high as the temperatures, with Tuscaloosa reaching triple digits the day prior to the third and final arrest.

On Friday, June 23, twenty-eight-year-old Elmore "Honey" Clark—a black man described as having a "shriveled and practically useless" arm—was found hiding beneath Big Sandy Bridge. Harden and Pippen had supposedly mentioned his name in connection with the murder, and as a result, he was taken into custody soon after. Despite the difficulties a man with a shriveled arm might have lifting a rock above his head and murdering a healthy twenty-one-year-old girl, representatives from the Tuscaloosa sheriff's department did not hesitate in confining him to a jail cell.

You Elmore Clark? a deputy called, cutting his way through the brambles, handcuffs in hand.

Yes, sir, I am.

Well, get out from that bridge then. We need to talk with you.

The following day's court proceedings more closely resembled an elaborate game of finger pointing than a courtroom. While fifteen-year-old Harden swore to have witnessed Pippen and Clark drag "the Maddox girl into a clump of bushes by the roadside" and "to have heard noises which convinced him that they raped and murdered her," Pippen denied the claim, placing the blame squarely on the newly arrested Clark.

Meanwhile, the sheriff's department had their own theory—that Clark and Pippen raped and murdered Vaudine while Harden functioned as a lookout at the side of the road. But despite their great efforts, the prosecution couldn't cobble together that particular version from the various versions at their disposal. The blame continued to pass from one to the next until eventually all three were indicted for murder.

The news of their indictments traveled north, and soon after, the International Labor Defense—a New York–based liberal-leaning defense organization—headed south, offering Pippen, Harden, and Clark a full arsenal of defense lawyers.

It's debatable whether or not the defendants requested their assistance, but it didn't matter.

The Northerners were invading.

Just months prior, in March 1933, the International Labor Defense legal team represented the nine black men charged in the Scottsboro case. The men were charged with brutally raping two white women while on a train from Chattanooga to Memphis, though much like in the Maddox case, the evidence remained spotty and circumstantial.

While the fear of black men raping white women had long struck a nerve within the white consciousness, the frequency with which it occurred was actually quite rare. "It is true that the actual danger of the Southern white woman's being violated by the Negro has always been comparatively small," wrote author W. J. Cash in 1941, arguing that it was far more likely for a white woman to be "struck by lightning."

Historian Bertram Wyatt-Brown agrees, noting, "The charge [of black men raping white women] was often patently fraudulent and other motives, such as fears provoked by black tendencies to independence, refusal to be servile, or signs of economic advance, were involved." In short, a rape charge was a catch-all that was sure to incite riotous behavior, and the I.L.D. fought to expose these fraudulent charges in the courtroom.

Despite their legal support, the Scottsboro Boys were initially found guilty and eight were sent to death row, though their death sentences were later reduced. Journalist Paul Peters, who was present in the courtroom when the verdicts were read, reported that, "At each death verdict, the court room burst into cheers. A band outside blares: 'There'll be a Hot Time in the Old Town Tonight!'"

Despite what initially appeared as a loss for the I.L.D., their role in the Scottsboro case granted them great notoriety within the legal world, and upon hearing of Harden, Pippen, and Clark's legal troubles, three representatives made their way to Tuscaloosa.

It would be understatement to say that the Northern lawyers were not welcome. In fact, Southern whites were wholeheartedly repulsed by the idea, refusing to allow Northern "Communists" to infiltrate their city and corrupt the sanctity of their courtroom, despite the fact that one of the three "Northern" lawyers actually resided in Birmingham. Citizens began establishing watch groups and writing letters to the *Tuscaloosa News* to express their frustration. Equally averse to the outside lawyers was the African-American community itself. So adamant, in fact, that over a dozen prominent African-American reverends addressed the problem in the July 31 issue of the *Tuscaloosa News*.

Perhaps fearing that the International Labor Defense—which actually *did* have clear ties to the Communist Party—would only litter the road to equality with greater obstacles, the reverends publicly decried the interference, claiming that they, too, didn't want "outside influences" intervening in the courtroom, believing that the "Christian integrity of the citizens of this community will see to it that justice is given in these cases."

I.L.D. organizer Louis Harper was said to have convinced the three accused men to consider outside lawyers affiliated with his organization, and while they initially agreed, Harden and Clark quickly recanted, though some sources note that Pippen remained firm in his desire for outside legal assistance.

The Southern Commission on the Study of Lynching reports that on July 31, Birmingham lawyer Frank B. Irvin informed Judge Foster that, "he and two New York lawyers, representing the International Labor Defense, had been retained by the defendants and would appear in their behalf when court convened next morning."

As promised, the International Labor Defense representatives arrived the following morning, gallivanting into a Tuscaloosa courtroom, perturbing all involved. Immediately, representatives for Harden and Clark testified that they hadn't requested I.L.D. assistance and, quite to the contrary, much preferred their current counsel. Pippen, as well as his parents, quickly agreed.

After much debate, Judge Henry Foster refused to recognize I.L.D. lawyers Frank Irvin, Irving Schwab, or Allan Taub, their role in the trial concluding before ever getting its start. While Tuscaloosa certainly didn't want outsiders interfering, Schwab's role as an attorney in the Scottsboro trial may have further prejudiced the courtroom against the I.L.D.

Judge Foster remained convinced that John McQueen, Fleetwood Rice, and Reuben Wright—the three local lawyers assigned to the case—were more than sufficient. The *Tuscaloosa News* noted that McQueen, Rice, and Wright were "generally regarded as among the leading attorneys in the state," McQueen even serving as president of the Alabama Bar Association prior to taking the case.

Despite Judge Foster's decision, the city remained furious over the I.L.D.'s brazen showiness and complete disregard for the Southern court system. Tuscaloosa's citizens interpreted the I.L.D.'s brash behavior as a direct insult to their town and their way of life—both unforgivable trespasses.

To make matters worse, two of the three lawyers were Jewish, which only furthered anti-Semitic sentiment around town. According to the *Tuscaloosa News,* prominent local Jewish merchant William P. Bloom took it upon himself to defuse the matter. In a letter to Rabbi Stephen S. Wise of New York, Bloom asked the rabbi to "exert his best efforts" to ensure that the International Labor Defense steered clear of Tuscaloosa. Bloom—who later played an integral role in passing the 1949 antimasking law in Alabama (making it a misdemeanor to appear in public wearing a mask and, in effect, disrupting the Ku Klux Klan's hooded trademark)—recognized the importance of siding with his city in order to protect Tuscaloosa's Jewish community and acted accordingly.

Yet Tuscaloosa citizens' frustration stemmed not from any political or religious group within the city limits but, rather, from the simple fact that Northern outsiders were attempting to assert themselves in a local matter. This wasn't the first time Southerners had fallen victim to outside influences; over the years, this pattern of Northern interference had become well cemented in the Southern mind. Many Southerners viewed the slavery issue as the first instance in which Northerners unnecessarily interceded into their lives and viewed reconstruction as a second transgression. This precedent left Southerners distrustful of outsiders and contributed to Southerners' negative feelings toward the International Labor Defense.

Tuscaloosa, in particular, had a reason to doubt the intentions of Northerners. In April 1865, General John T. Croxton of the Union Army marched 2,600 white soldiers (as well as many African-Americans who joined them) across the Black Warrior River and onto Tuscaloosa's shores. The university campus (a military school at the time) was soon burned, except for four buildings that managed to withstand the flames. One famous story recounts Professor Andrew DeLoffre's valiant attempt at saving the university's prestigious library and the rare books within, though Croxton refused the request, fulfilling his orders to torch it alongside the other more military-oriented structures. The action seemed only to add insult to injury—a physical display of the destruction of Southern culture by the Northern invaders. It was a wound that had yet to heal, and sixty-eight years after the university's burning, this latest intrusion of Northerners did not sit well with the citizens of 1933.

Clarence Cason reports that after the I.L.D. lawyers entered the courtroom, "several hundred persons had gathered outside the courthouse to mumble to each other about those Communists from the North." The mob's hatred toward the three blacks subsided as they redirected their fury to the "three little Jewish lawyers being paid to spread ideas of social equality among the Alabama Negroes."

Cason quotes Judge Foster, who solidified this claim, explaining to reporters that, "There is no feeling against the Negroes here, and guards were not needed to protect the defendants."

In actuality, the guards were needed to protect the Northern lawyers, instead.

Fearing that the I.L.D. might cause a second mob, the governor called in the National Guard, which immediately set to work dispersing the growing crowds by launching tear gas into the throngs of gatherers. Well aware of the excitement brewing in the streets, the judge ordered those inside the courtroom to stay put, hoping the mob would subside by the time the three I.L.D. lawyers left to catch their afternoon train. But as the violence continued to mount, the Northern lawyers had no choice but to disguise themselves in an attempt to sneak over to the county jail, at which point they were given a police escort to Greensboro Avenue, where they boarded their train at the Southern Railway station.

The I.L.D. lawyers left soon after their arrival, though their presence lingered, leaving a trail of anxiety long after the locomotive smoke dissipated.

The I.L.D.'s short-lived trip to Tuscaloosa stirred the town into a frenzy, sending whites into fits in which they claimed Northern Communists were corrupting their loyal Negro citizens.

An August 3 headline in the *Tuscaloosa News* read: "I.L.D. Interference Costs State and County $1500"—a figure far more accurate than Tuscaloosa might have hoped.

The city footed a $500 bill while the state hefted twice that amount, the cost of transporting sixty-six National Guardsmen from Fort McClellan to Tuscaloosa, one hundred and twenty miles to the west. It was a high price to pay to ensure the safety of three Communist lawyers who, according to the Tuscaloosa courtroom, had no business interfering with local issues in the first place.

Many concurred that the witch hunt that followed was a direct result of the I.L.D.'s trip.

While various frenzied reports decried the influx of Communists in Tuscaloosa, one levelheaded article more accurately assessed the reality of the situation: "Despite the earnest statements of officials and leading white citizens, who seem to have thoroughly convinced themselves that Communists [are] all over the country-side . . . persistent inquiry reveal[s] only meager traces of their presence."

And yet, regardless of facts, much of the white citizenry of Tuscaloosa remained convinced that Communists had infiltrated every arena of city life, that their encroachment was rampant, and in the most extreme case, that groups of carpetbaggers were actually advising African-Americans to "take liberties with white women."

Sheriff Shamblin capitalized on the citizens' fears, asking residents to report any strangers they happened to spot around town.

It was as if the entire city had suddenly lost sight of the original charges.

Tuscaloosa had a murderer on its hands (or according to Sheriff Shamblin, three murderers, all of whom were in custody), yet Vaudine Maddox's death opened the doors to far more repressed fears—the incursion of Northern "strangers" and "Communists"—fears that had been left to fester since Reconstruction.

Civil unrest continued to grow, and while the trial for Harden, Pippen, and Clark had been set for August 22, rumors began circulating of a lynching to take place on Saturday, August 12, ten days prior to the court date.

The circuit judge caught wind of these rumors, and at 7:00 p.m. on Saturday, August 12, he decided to transport the three prisoners to Birmingham once more to minimize their risk. He left the task to three deputies—R. M. Pate, N. W. Holman, and W. I. Huff—though when the judge phoned at 9:00 p.m., he was baffled to learn that the prisoners had not yet been transported. All the while, the unnecessarily long discussion that preceded the prisoners' relocation allowed the townspeople's fervor to grow just beyond the jail doors.

Tuscaloosa's citizens were angry and anxious to act, and thanks in part to the seemingly lackadaisical attitude of the sheriff's deputies, their opportunity was unfolding.

That same year, 1933, James Harmon Chadbourn published *Lynching and the Law,* dedicating an entire chapter to the transferring of prisoners in which he concluded, "The fewer technical formalities that are necessary to secure removal, the better the statute is for expeditious results. On this basis, the type of law which empowers the sheriff to act on his own initiative seems best."

Tuscaloosa's deputies managed the opposite, inhibiting the process rather than expediting anything. While the circuit judge swiftly gave the orders, deputies Pate, Holman, and Huff took their time transporting the men, dragging what should have been a quick-clipped ninety-minute drive into a leisurely two-and-a-half-hour journey. Their car puttered north along the road, their headlights cutting through the heavy darkness. After two and a half hours, they had only managed to make it thirty miles outside of Tuscaloosa, indicating that the deputies drove at approximately ten miles per hour, suspiciously below the speed limit. The officers' reported that they took a "circuitous route," though their rationale remains unclear. Prior to the prisoners' leaving, four other deputies had driven ahead in order to ensure the road was clear for transport.

The deputies failed miserably.

Halfway into their trip, the transport officers were met by two cars, their headlights blinding. A twelve-person mob blocked the road, their faces covered with black masks, small eyeholes punched through the fabric. The men shifted their weight from one foot to the other, brandishing their guns.

As the deputies stepped from their car into the night, one of the masked men spoke.

"We want those niggers and we are going to have them, and we don't want any argument about it."

The deputies hesitated, but Pippen, Harden, and Clark—all handcuffed together—obediently climbed from one car to the next, settling into the seats.

"Now drive on to Birmingham," one of the masked men ordered, "and don't stop until you get there. Don't turn around."

The deputies returned to their car, driving a mile down the road toward Birmingham before hurrying back to Tuscaloosa.

They returned to the sheriff's department at 1:30 a.m. The deputies immediately spread word of the abducted prisoners and search parties began to assemble, preparing to comb the Alabama countryside, including Vaudine Maddox's murder site in Big Sandy, where officers believed the mob might exact their revenge. The searchers divided into separate cars before beginning the painstaking process of marching through the tall grass along the roadways, keeping their eyes to the ground for any traces of struggle. Despite their efforts, their search proved fruitless until 10:00 a.m. the following morning, when the bullet-riddled bodies of A. T. Harden and Dan Pippen Jr. were discovered approximately seven miles from where they were first appre-hended, their blood dried to their clothing. Most likely, the search party would have continued throughout the day if it weren't for a tip from a passing motorist who reported what he mistook as "two drunken negroes lying near the roadside." According to the *Tuscaloosa News,* their bodies were found "100 yards from the Tuscaloosa County line," conveniently placing the crime in Bibb County's jurisdiction, though a joint investigation was eventually launched.

While Harden and Pippen's bodies were immediately recovered, re-markably, Honey Clark's was not among them.

The search continued, though Clark was not found until Monday, alive but injured, and recuperating from three gunshots wounds in a black woman's cabin outside of Vance, ten miles from where Harden and Pippen's bodies were discovered.

In the thirty-six hours following the executions, an injured Clark limped between twelve to sixteen miles through the wilderness before stumbling across the woman's cabin. Clark's injuries were so serious that the woman called upon a neighbor to walk twenty-five miles back to Tuscaloosa for medical aid. African-American doctor B. H. Mitchell was summoned, and the deputies recovered Clark soon after, though not before the I.L.D. contacted President Roosevelt requesting fed-eral protection for the lone survivor of the assault. However, the re-quest was superfluous; this time around, Judge Foster called in the Na-tional Guard to ensure Clark's safety. One hundred and twenty soldiers began patrolling the streets, giving the courthouse "the appearance of a military fort" according to the Southern Commission on the Study of Lynching.

No mob dared challenge the soldiers.

Barbed wire was stretched on all sides of the courthouse, transform-ing the quaint Southern town into a military complex. The towns-people watched helplessly as uniformed men overtook Tuscaloosa, blocking off city streets until Clark was called to court to recount the events of August 12 to a special grand jury three days after his capture.

Once on the stand, a nervous Clark explained the night to the best of his memory.

"Two cars were standing in the road," he recalled, "one of them was kind of dimmed and cut off just before they got to us . . . They drove up on in front and to the side of us too . . . I seen the pistols."

He went on to explain how they were forced from the police car and ordered to get into the backseat of one of the mob's two vehicles, how they sat quietly while the men proceeded to fix a punctured tire.

"They asked A. T. who killed the girl and A. T. said Dan was the one killed the girl," Clark testified. "They asked him how he knew he killed her he said, 'I was with him,' and he asked who all was with him and he said, 'no one but me and Dan' . . . That was all that happened in the way of talking."

The three young black men were lined up in the dark as the mob aimed their guns and fired. The shots rang out, piercing the night, and Clark felt the hot shrapnel tear into his arm. He collapsed beneath Harden and Pippen's lifeless bodies, blacked out, and when he awoke sometime later, the mob had vanished.

He tried reorienting himself, staring blurry-eyed into the field as his arm continued to throb. He sat up, his hand falling to a nearby pine knot. Finding himself handcuffed to a dead body, he took the pine knot and began hitting the weak joint of the cuff.

"[The cuffs] kind of hurt my hand," Clark admitted, "and something was telling me if you don't get them off them folks will come back and kill you too. I hit the handcuff right smart. After I got loose I asked the Lord to bring me back to Tuscaloosa."

SECOND LOOP
A CHALLENGE

Tuscaloosa, August–October 1933

A matter of profound humiliation.

Despite speculation that the three Tuscaloosa deputies not only had prior knowledge of the mob but actively took part in the murders, they were not convicted of any wrongdoing. Deputy R. M. Pate, in particular, had a reputation for being "quick on the trigger, where Negroes [were] involved," a reputation he upheld just days later by killing twenty-four-year-old Jack Pruitt, a black man who supposedly made threats to a white farmer before running toward the officer with a club. While author Clarence Cason doesn't refer to Pruitt by name, he makes note of the black man shot "within a few hundred yards of the fourth tee of the Tuscaloosa Country Club." Pate was rumored to have killed about a dozen blacks at the time of the lynchings, and those who knew him suspected he was fully aware of the unfortunate events that befell the men he was entrusted to protect.

Meanwhile, the mob was found as innocent as the deputies.

In a *Tuscaloosa News* editorial printed the day following the lynching, one writer noted that Pippen and Harden weren't victims of the mob, but rather, of the International Labor Defense's intrusiveness.

"There was a threat of grave disorder in Tuscaloosa over this case and it all is the fault of the International Labor Defense," agreed Judge Foster in the *Birmingham Post*. "If they had stayed out of this case I am confident there would have been no lynchings."

Another editorial claimed that Northern carpetbaggers had disrupted the tenuous balance struck between Southern whites and blacks years before, a silent code of conduct in which alleged rape and murder were recognized as offenses punishable by death whenever the mob saw fit.

"May God forgive the carpet baggers of today who returned this foul thing [lynching] to our midst—human hearts cannot," one letter writer asserted. "Dan Pippen and A. T. Harden, two young Negroes accused of the murder of a white girl, lie dead."

Another editorial placed the blame on the I.L.D. even more pointedly.

"[T]he maggoty beaks of the belled buzzards of the International Labor Defense League are stained with the blood of the three Negro boys whose torn bodies this morning lay in newly-turned graves! The International Labor Defense League has at last accomplished what it has long sought. It has made martyrs of three Alabama defendants in a criminal case—dead martyr to a mock Cause."

The writer went on to claim that neither Harden nor Pippen nor Clark wanted anything more than a fair trial, "[b]ut the boys' pleas failed to stop the belled buzzards. They continued to circle over Alabama and Tuscaloosa."

While the writer admitted the city's own implication in the murders, he went on to decry the "belled buzzards" who continued leaving "vermin in their path across the state" and worse still, "blood on the Great Seal of Alabama."

After acknowledging his own "closeness" to Tuscaloosa made it difficult to offer a "completely detached analysis," Clarence Cason admitted that he, too, believed that, "none of the lynchings would have taken place had it not been for the resentment directly created by the three Communist lawyers who deliberately irritated a disturbed situation by their offensive presence."

The citizens of Tuscaloosa concurred.

Citizens refused to blame either the deputies or the mob, and instead, managed to shift the blame entirely on what they perceived as a Northern, Communist threat. It was easier to blame outsiders than their neighbors, regardless of skin color. When taken together, these editorials point to the true cause of the violence: Tuscaloosa citizens lynched two black men, not because of any particular crime, but to send a message that New York lawyers were not to interfere with Southern issues of race. However, the unintended consequence of sending such a message was that they were also informing the country that lawlessness had overtaken the town.

A special grand jury was called to investigate the violence, and while the judge wholeheartedly condemned the mob's actions, the surprise came during Honey Clark's testimony.

Perhaps all too aware of the consequences of his statement, Clark offered as little blame as possible, refusing to point fingers and, instead, defended the deputies, claiming that the mob had swiftly overtaken them through no fault of their own.

"[The mob] had the guns on Mr. Pate and these other men and they had to turn us over to these men," Clark testified. "When we first stopped Mr. Pate got his gun and the others, too, but they could not do anything and had to give us up."

It was the answer the courtroom most wanted to hear—that the integrity of the sheriff's department remained intact, that the deputies acted heroically in the face of mortal danger.

Despite Alabama Attorney General Thomas Knight Jr.'s attempts to recess, Judge Foster demanded the lynching investigation proceed uninterrupted. It stretched throughout August and September, Judge Foster requiring that the jury actually visit the physical locations where the mob apprehended Pippen, Harden, and Clark, as well as the location where they were shot. Little evidence remained, though Cason noted, "There might have been more bullets for the ballistic experts to examine had it not been for the fact that farmers living near the scene of the lynching had cut some of them into little mementos of the occasion." As a result, the grand jury ordered Dan Pippen Jr.'s body be exhumed in order to remove a bullet from his abdomen, which they believed could assist in the investigation. A bullet was also removed from Clark's shoulder, and a Birmingham ballistics expert was called in to determine if the bullets could shed new light on the case, though his findings remain unknown.

Alabama Attorney General Thomas Knight Jr. (a prosecutor who had faced off against the I.L.D. in the Scottsboro case) offered his expertise in the Tuscaloosa investigation as well, though upon entering the courtroom on September 5, Chief Deputy Sheriff Gilbert's high-powered rifle—which he'd haphazardly left on the courtroom floor beside his feet with the safety off—accidentally discharged, not only shooting Knight in the heel, but managing to injure Gilbert's foot as well.

It was just one of the many ironies of the investigation.

While it's uncertain exactly what role—if any—Tuscaloosa's law enforcement and court system played in the murders of Dan Pippen Jr. and A. T. Harden, they had, at least in one instance, quite literally shot themselves in the feet.

On October 2, the grand jury investigation of the lynchings returned a "No Bill," concluding that there was not sufficient evidence to convict the mob responsible for shooting and killing two prisoners of the state.

When reading their position, the grand jury praised virtually everyone involved in the unsuccessful efforts to unmask the mob.

"We also wish to say that we have had no evidence introduced which in anyway causes us to lose our faith and confidence in [Sheriff] Mr. Fayette Shamblin," they concluded, perhaps muddying their objectivity in the process.

Next, they went on to thank the attorney general and the circuit solicitor for their fine attempts at tracking down the culprits, though not a single culprit was ever held accountable.

As one writer put it, "So all the officials were exonerated, all the lynchers were left unmolested—and nobody was surprised at the outcome."

Yet one mystery remained: Why had Pippen and Harden been riddled with bullets while Clark escaped virtually unscathed?

The *Tuscaloosa News* suggested that the mob organized a midnight trial, noting that Clark's life was spared because the mob had found Clark innocent, that his strong alibi was proof enough for his release.

It's a difficult scene to envision: a lynch mob conducting a midnight trial and achieving what the courtroom could not—full confessions from Pippen and Harden while exonerating Clark.

However, the midnight trial theory was soon disproved.

As Clark later described, the masked men simply asked who had killed Vaudine Maddox and Harden had pointed to Pippen while Clark maintained his innocence.

The mob didn't care.

They fired on all three.

Clark collapsed directly beneath Pippen's body, shielding himself from further injury.

Elmore "Honey" Clark wasn't spared by the mob; he simply benefited by its unwillingness to check for a pulse.

A month later, Dennis Cross, a forty-nine-year-old paralytic black man, was charged with tearing a dress and attempting to attack Alice

Johnson, an eighteen-year-old female from a poor white family. Cross was a well-known figure around town, a former coal worker whose paralysis was the result of a stroke suffered four years prior. Meanwhile, Alice Johnson had her own reputation—one of wrongful accusations.

On September 12, she marched dutifully into the Tuscaloosa Emergency Relief office and pointed to nearby Cross, identifying him as her attacker.

Yet, as the Southern Commission on the Study of Lynching reported, "it is a matter of fact that Dennis Cross was unable to run; that his brother had dressed and undressed him for four years; that his paralysis . . . made it highly improbable that he was capable of the crime implied by the woman's accusations."

Ironically, a similar situation had arisen just months prior, when Honey Clark was accused of murdering Vaudine Maddox, while he, too, had an unworkable limb.

Both stories are eerily familiar to the one Harper Lee dreamed up in her landmark literary debut, *To Kill a Mockingbird*. In the novel, a crippled black man named Tom Robinson is accused of raping Mayella Ewell—a nineteen-year-old female who was also from "a very poor local white family"—despite the fact that Robinson's own paralysis rendered the crime implausible. We can only speculate whether Lee, who attended The University of Alabama twelve years after these incidents, ever caught wind of these tales and incorporated them into her work.

However, one crucial difference between fact and fiction is that in Lee's novel, Atticus Finch stands guard over the jailhouse on the night of Tom Robinson's attempted lynching while Scout, Jem, and Dill assist by employing their innocence to shame the mob back into the shadows.

Unfortunately for Dennis Cross, no innocent children or morally unshakable lawyers jumped to his defense on the last night of his life.

At 2:00 a.m. on Sunday, September 24, Cross was roused from his bed by seven white men who claimed to be police officers, informing him that he needed to pay a larger bond, and that they would gladly escort him to the courthouse to take care of the matter.

Instead, they drove Cross to a wooded area near the Black Warrior River—the site of the alleged assault on Alice Johnson—where he was shot four times, murdered for allegedly tearing a dress.

In *A Rage for Order,* Joel Williamson writes, "from the white point of view, one might say that the Negro-as-scapegoat has been one of the nation's most valuable renewable resources. He can be used again and yet again, and never wear out."

Throughout the summer of 1933, the violent acts that occurred in and around Tuscaloosa validated Williamson's claim, though Harden and Pippen's unjustifiable murders also spurred the state's more progressive voices to sound off in protest. Public opinion began to shift following the Cross lynching, and the epidemic of vigilante justice was more than many citizens could swallow, including Governor B. M. Miller, who offered a $400 reward along with this statement condemning the most recent lynching: "This offense on its reported face is so heinous, that without call from an official of the county, this reward of $400 is offered for the arrest and conviction of the offenders . . . The law must be obeyed, if not, the guilty must be punished."

The *Birmingham News* agreed.

"For the second time within little more than a month, Alabama is put to shame by a lynching. And again it is Tuscaloosa County that is the scene of the outrage."

The *Birmingham Post* added additional pressure, claiming that if "the sheriff of Tuscaloosa County and the three deputies he named to escort Dan Pippen and A. T. Harden to Birmingham had been courageous and alert in the discharge of their sworn duty, there would have been no lynching."

A second grand jury was called just a week after the first, though once again, they failed to bring anyone to justice, placing the blame on a "lack of adequate detective talent."

Throughout the state, women's groups made their disgust known in letters to the governor, in which they stated "the majesty of the law [has been] shamefully outraged within our beloved commonwealth," and that the recent upswing in violence was a "matter of profound humiliation to every law abiding citizen of intelligence."

Following their wives' lead, men's groups wrote, "Whatever the crimes of the prisoners, they were awaiting trial under the laws of the state, and all outside interference had been carefully excluded by the court. The majesty of the state cannot yield to lynch law."

Yet John Temple Graves, II, a columnist for the *Birmingham Age-Herald*, offered the most scathing critique of all, calling the Cross lynching "one of the most shameful affairs with which Alabama has ever had to deal," arguing that only "genuine efforts" would lead to justice. According to a 1946 issue of *Time* magazine, Graves's column, "This Morning," had appeared on the front page of the *Birmingham Age-Herald* for seventeen years, solidifying him as a man "in favor of Southern chivalry, Birmingham-made steel, free enterprise . . . and segregation of Negroes." Yet even the unapologetic segregationist was offended by the racial violence, demanding that "genuine efforts" be given to solve the heinous crime.

By 1933, the entire county was mired in so many personal interests that any attempt at genuine efforts seemed far beyond its reach. The law—as well as the courts set up to uphold it—were rendered useless by what many whites determined was a racial obligation to their own.

After receiving heat from national papers, the *Tuscaloosa News* took matters into its own hands, sounding the call for reform by running a four-column front page editorial, asking, "Shall We Accept the Challenge?"

The editorial claimed that the I.L.D. had "inflamed the people to such a point that the community was tense with fear of racial disorders" and that when "the handful of men took the matter into their own hands . . . a certain relief was undeniably felt by even the most thoughtful and law-abiding of our citizens."

Yet it continued: "But the International Labor Defense cannot be blamed for the murder of Dennis Cross."

Despite efforts to place the blame for the city's renewed violence squarely on the shoulders of outside interference, the *Tuscaloosa News* was the first to acknowledge that at least a portion of the violence had festered from within.

The editorial called upon citizens, social clubs, churches, and the Tuscaloosa Bar Association to fight for a return to order. It was a skillfully written maneuver that allowed the city to save face by placing the power of reform easily within their reach. Those who had committed the violence were now in a position to be praised for halting future attempts; their redemption was their own.

Surprisingly, much of the Tuscaloosa community bought into it. The very people who just days before had taken pride in their city's ability to keep the Northerners at bay underwent a miraculous change of heart. Citizens began defending all those weaker than themselves in exchange for some semblance of returning honor to their city.

Days later, the *Tuscaloosa News* reported, "The Rotary Club, the Kiwanis Club, the Civitan Club, the Exchange Club, the Chamber of Commerce, the Daughters of the American Revolution, the American Legion" and scores of other organizations had all "pledged their full support" in scrubbing clean Tuscaloosa's violent past.

"Never before in the history of this newspaper had any editorial or other article received such a spontaneous, spirited and united response from the citizens of the community," claimed one newspaper official. The publisher was rumored to have received so many congratulatory calls that he had to "remove the receiver from his home at midnight in order to permit sleep."

As promised, swift action followed.

The County Council Against Crime was organized and immediately set to work passing resolutions and forming specific plans of action committed to halting the violence. They requested church services focused on community civility, as well as slideshows in local theaters addressing messages such as "(a.) Violence always hurts a community. (b.) Tuscaloosa is 'on the spot' before the eyes of the world. (c.) There must be no more violence in Tuscaloosa."

Tuscaloosa was not accustomed to receiving such an audience, and the city reveled in its opportunity to prove to the nation that a small Southern town could serve as the model of civility.

Yet despite the city's growing enthusiasm, the County Council Against Crime soon found itself up against a rival group, the Citizens Protective League, whose main objective was to protect white citizens against unnamed threats, though their methods were questionable. They called themselves "Communist hunters" though they often confused Communists with blacks.

One report claimed that in the outlying areas between Tuscaloosa and Moundville masked men—most likely Citizens Protective League members—"maintained a reign of terror," oftentimes breaking into African-Americans' homes and discharging firearms as a scare tactic.

One black man recounted waking to find robed figures gathered around his bed like specters. He leapt through a window and was fired at multiple times as he disappeared into the night.

Despite their wildly different objectives, the Citizens Protective League had a difficult time separating their goals from those of the County Council Against Crime. In the October 8 issue of the *Tuscaloosa News* they attempted to make their aim clear: "to protect the community from the 'dastardly insults of the I.L.D.'"

However, virtually all signs of I.L.D. involvement in Tuscaloosa had dissipated months before when the three lawyers boarded the train. Nevertheless, the Citizens Protective League felt it their civic duty to continue to "combat [Communists'] sinister activities in our county with all honorable means that can be mustered at our command."

Placing the focus on Northern invaders rather than their own racial biases allowed the citizens to ignore the issue that would continue to haunt them throughout the Civil Rights Movement. Rather than confronting the obvious problem, deflection allowed for a blind-eye approach to reform.

The editorial from the Citizens Protective League continued: "We agree with all normal thinking people that lynch law must be condemned as it is degrading and barbarous, with tendencies to uproot and undermine the fundamental principles of civilization. Still we must ever be mindful of the human element responsible for such occurrences. When our neighbors' wives or daughters are brutally attacked and murdered, having been victims of the atrocious crimes executed by white or black to satisfy their doggish lust, we wonder if our homes will not be next."

The phrase "white or black" managed to deemphasize the Citizens Protective League's racial overtones, leading the community to believe that their vigilante efforts did not necessarily stop at the color line.

The great irony is that many associated with the County Council Against Crime found themselves equally connected with the Citizens Protective League. Author Clarence Cason points out this hypocritical behavior, noting that, "The southern conscience is unruffled by the act of lifting a glass with one hand and gesturing for prohibition in the other."

In short, citizens were betting on both horses, certain one or the other would soon win out, and everyone wanted to stand with the victor.

Tuscaloosa's sudden progressive shift seemed too good to be true.

And in all actuality, it was.

Throughout the first week of October, editorials in the *Tuscaloosa News* praised the town for its recent change of heart, giving Tuscaloosa's citizens reason to feel proud again. And while it seemed counterproductive to their recent call for order, even the Citizens Protective League was publicly commended for their "great service" in managing to run "down rumors of all kind . . . without any compensation."

While the County Council Against Crime and Citizens Protective League both pledged to fight to protect Tuscaloosa's citizens, the tactics by which they chose to wage their wars were quite different. But as time revealed, the County Council Against Crime's church sermons, slideshows, and letter-writing campaigns proved far less effective than the more archaic weapons: masked men, guns, and a propensity for violence.

Tuscaloosa was no stranger to violence, though it hadn't always revealed itself by way of gunfire and lynching ropes. Equally dangerous was the First Amendment and a man and his printing press.

Tuscaloosa's first incarnation of the Ku Klux Klan organized in 1868, though the twenty or so men held their meetings outside the city, in nearby Sipsy Swamp. There, the group began to multiply, primarily by the efforts of Grand Giant and *Independent Monitor* editor, Ryland Randolph, whose publication's motto was: "The White Man—Right or Wrong—Still, the White Man."

"He made a brave fight for the county in those dark days: no one was truer to the white man's cause than he," wrote University of Alabama student Gladys Ward in her 1932 thesis. "For a period conservative people of the Democratic party fairly idolized him."

He became known as the "fighting editor," not only because of the pair of derringer pistols, double-barrel shotgun, and spring blade knife that were casually strewn across his desk, but also due to his vitriolic articles. Ward wrote that the Klan's purpose was to "terrorize and punish insolent negroes and disreputable whites"—a responsibility Randolph did not take lightly. The *Independent Monitor* became his greatest weapon—a mouthpiece to the community—and he often filled its pages with "Blacks Lists" which, as Ward noted, publicly decried "negroes who were especially odious and incendiary."

On March 28, 1868, Randolph overheard a raucous crowd gathering in the streets. Upon witnessing two black men beating a white man, he reached for his knife and began repeatedly stabbing African-American Balus Eddins, who had allegedly rushed him. After issuing several well-placed stabs, Randolph promptly wiped the blood from his knife onto his shoe and strolled back to his newspaper room. While his friends begged him to skip town—warning that angry blacks were gathering—Randolph refused, noting that "the good he had done . . . would be undone if he ran way."

Soon after, he was taken to Selma to stand trial under a military commission, though he was found not guilty. Ward described the hero's welcome he received upon riding back to Tuscaloosa a free man: "As they approached town, all the church bells began to ring . . . People crowded around his carriage . . . many enthusiastic ladies following behind . . . the foremost citizens made speeches welcoming him home and commending him for upholding the white man's cause so gallantly."

After stabbing Balus Eddins—which, according to Ward, Randolph considered "the proudest act of his life"—Randolph became even more brazen in employing his newspaper as a means to threaten both African-Americans and Northern carpetbaggers. No event better supports this than Randolph's battle against The University of Alabama, whose board of regents had hired a Northern preacher named A. S. Lakin to serve as its president following the Civil War. State Superintendent Dr. N. B. Cloud and A. S. Lakin made their way to Tuscaloosa, though they were pelted with insults along the way. Randolph took matters into his own hands, printing a now infamous woodcut depicting two white men hanging from a tree, one carrying a suitcase labeled "Ohio" (from where Lakin had come) while, just ahead, a horse with the letters "KKK" continues trotting forward.

Lakin observed the woodcut while flipping through the *Monitor*'s pages and swiftly resigned.

When the board of regents tried to hire yet another Northern preacher, R. D. Harper, Randolph increased his threats, declaring that he preferred that the university close down rather than be ruled by a scalawag. The board of regents took Randolph seriously and, in August 1869, passed a resolution which said: "Whereas the best interests of the State University and its future success demand its removal from its present site in Tuskaloosa [sic] and located elsewhere, [t]herefore be it resolved . . . to remove said university at the earliest moment practical."

The decision was later overturned, though for a brief moment, the power of Ryland Randolph's *Independent Monitor* nearly closed the university's Tuscaloosa doors once and for all.

A. S. Lakin and R. D. Harper's short-lived experience at The University of Alabama foreshadowed what many white Southerners feared when the I.L.D. strode into town over sixty years later—a town overrun by Northern intellectuals.

Ryland Randolph's caustic language and pointed knives were a beginning—but not an end—to the violence that would continue far into Tuscaloosa's future.

While it's difficult to track Alabama's racial violence, undoubtedly it's rooted as far back as the first slave ships' arrivals at the Mobile docks. Glenn Feldman offers the most comprehensive study on this particular breed of violence, citing 1819 as the year of Alabama's first official lynching. Feldman contends that this practice was "probably a rarer occurrence before the Civil War than after," because "blacks enjoyed a protective status that they lost after 1865." Simply put, white slave owners didn't want their property "chased and killed by a mob of their neighbors," though after the slaves were set free, whites no longer felt the need to protect them. It wasn't a matter of morality but economics—their property had lost its value.

Even more troubling, however, was that in 1868—the same year the Ku Klux Klan emerged in Tuscaloosa County—the state of Alabama passed antilynching legislation that punished the perpetrators of mob violence, though this legislation was later repealed. In 1933, James Harmon Chadbourn wrote that while the "exact dates of repeal and the reasons actuating it have not been discovered," most likely due to unpopular reconstruction efforts, Alabama actually took a significant leap backward by repealing their previous legislation, stopping just short of what some might broadly interpret as the state-sanctioned murder of blacks.

As a result, throughout the 1890s, Alabama became the nation's leader in lynchings, boasting a stupefying one hundred and seventy-seven victims. "When lynching was most popular," Feldman writes, "Alabamians lynched most." He notes the irony as well—that despite the record-breaking violence, this time period in American history is called the Progressive Era.

But perhaps the most noteworthy statistic is not the number of casualties, but rather, their racial makeup. In the 1890s, "70 percent of the victims in both Alabama and the United States . . . were black," writes Feldman. "After 1900 the percentages were about 90 percent for the nation and 95 percent for Alabama."

The trend was clear: Lynchings had become directly tied to race.

From 1889 to 1921, Tuscaloosa County claimed six lynchings, Birmingham's Jefferson County fourteen, while Mobile County rested comfortably at twelve. As Feldman notes, at the state level, of the one hundred and thirty-eight lynchings that occurred between 1900 and 1921, only five of the victims were white.

Alabama significantly contributed to the nation's lynching statistics, and as a result of the negative publicity the state had endured, a few politicians took up the call to end lynching once and for all. Believing a lack of accountability from local authorities to be the root of the problem, Governor Emmet O'Neal (1911–1915) attempted to enforce the Alabama Constitution, which stated "whenever any prisoner is taken from jail, or from the custody of any sheriff or his deputy and put to death or suffers grievous bodily harm, owing to the neglect, connivance, cowardice, or other grave fault of the sheriff, such sheriff may be impeached." Yet when Governor O'Neal tested this on a negligent sheriff from Bullock County, Chadbourn reports, "A petition signed by 2,879 persons, many of them the Governor's political supporters, was presented to seek withdrawal of the proceedings."

The mandate was good in theory, just not in practice.

Nevertheless, small signs of progress were visible, leading Feldman to conclude, "By 1921 lynching was not a rarity in Alabama; yet it was far from the common occurrence that it had once been."

But less than a decade later, the pendulum of violence would swing back.

From the spring of 1931 through October of '33, Tuscaloosa County recorded seventy murders—nearly two a month for a county whose population was approximately 65,000. Tuscaloosa's homicide rate was keeping pace with Memphis and Atlanta—"the most murderous cities in the country" according to the Southern Commission on the Study of Lynching. Equally shocking was the lack of accountability. "In the seventy capital cases mentioned above," the Commission reports, "not one death sentence has been imposed, and only one sentence of life imprisonment."

There were many theories for this heightened violence, including politics and economics, but above all else was simply the prejudices many whites still held toward blacks, believing blacks were intellectually inferior and, therefore, "ordained to a position of subservience and servitude." Many whites felt it "unnecessary to provide for [them] either the educational opportunities, the health facilities, or the police protection which it provides for the white person." This rationale, coupled with an insufficient court system, created an environment in which violence could flourish.

The University of Alabama remained suspiciously quiet throughout the city's sudden surge in racial violence. Rather than leading the charge for reform, it was said to have "lived quite within itself." Not only did the university remain silent, but it also offered few, if any, educational opportunities for local citizens. As proof of this failure to act, the literacy rate for whites in Tuscaloosa County ranked lower than the rest of the state, regardless of the vast educational resources at the city's doorstep. The 1933 back-to-school issue of the university paper, *The Crimson White,* made no mention of the recent surge in violence throughout the community, preferring to report on the upcoming football season and what movies were playing at the Bama Theatre.

However, one voice from the university did make itself heard above the silence, and it belonged to Professor J. R. Steelman, whose liberal leanings and investigations into the racial violence spurred a mob of Klansmen to approach him one night, accusing him of Communist ties. As writer Robin Kelley reports, "Although Steelman vigorously denied the charge, hostility toward him and his family forced him to leave the county." However, the move proved beneficial to Steelman, and after a stint at Alabama College in Montevallo, he was offered a job at the United States Conciliation Service, though he eventually rose to become President Harry Truman's assistant, a job in many ways similar to a modern chief of staff. Indirectly, the Klan's threats propelled him to the White House, making him one of the president's closest advisors.

In the fall of 1933, the Southern Commission on the Study of Lynching was asked, in light of the murderous summer, to investigate what caused the sudden uptick in violence. The result was a report entitled *The Plight of Tuscaloosa: A Case Study of Conditions in Tuscaloosa*

County, Alabama, 1933—from which many of these details were derived.

The report concluded that the violence stemmed from Tuscaloosa's awkward transition from a small country town to an overgrown country town. The commission described Tuscaloosa's streets as "filled with loitering whites and Negroes from the coal mines and abandoned farms" and that "[t]hese people live largely from public funds."

Further, it claimed that Communism was actually "Tuscaloosa's scapegoat," and that if Tuscaloosa's citizens were "really afraid of Communism, its best defense would lie in extending to Negroes full protection under the law."

"Even had these rumors [of a Communist threat] been true," the report continued, "they would have afforded no justification for an orgy of murder and intimidation."

But it noted a silver lining, as well.

"Tuscaloosa has some people who are thoroughly displeased with the recent mob outbreaks, lynchings, [and] futile grand jury investigations . . . this hopeful minority, so far largely inarticulate, can get the community to deal frankly and constructively with the unwholesome . . . factors which produced the recent mob murders, community hysteria, and official incompetence."

While the report remained vague on exactly what those unwholesome factors might be, undoubtedly it included issues of both race as well as xenophobia. For some Tuscaloosa citizens, the only thing worse than a black or a Northerner was a black Northerner, which often spelled "Communist" for the anxiety-stricken citizens (though white Jewish Northerners also fit the bill). While the city was only marginally successful in dealing "frankly and constructively" with the racial issues that had long been embedded within the town, the problem was acknowledged all the same. And while the city's breakneck speed of reform began to slow, it did not stall out completely.

In the end, local prosecutors took the greatest hit, though the blame also fell to the Supreme Court of Alabama, the Commission on the Study of Lynching charging it to fulfill its "obligation . . . to impeach officers who signally fail of their duty." The city's "good ol' boys' club" could no longer handle these issues in-house, though the commission's call for the removal of public officials was met with varied success.

Unfortunately, the robust debate that directly followed the terror of Tuscaloosa's summer of 1933 did little to halt the racially motivated lynchings that would continue to plague the state.

Over time, the barbaric practice began to subside, though not before a final hanging occurred nearly fifty years later, in 1981.

One cool March night, nineteen-year-old Michael Donald headed out of his sister's home for a pack of cigarettes.

He was found the next morning, dangling from a tree.

THIRD LOOP
A MOTEL SWIMMING POOL

Birmingham, November 29, 1979

My name is Robert.

November 29, 1979, was an unseasonably cold day in Birmingham, Alabama. A high of thirty-eight degrees left the city shivering; men and women walking hastily down the sidewalks, burrowing their hands in their pockets. For most, Birmingham represented a Southern hub of industry—particularly iron and steel—though for Josephus Anderson, who had arrived days before, it was just another heist.

At 3:30 p.m., thirty-seven-year-old Josephus Anderson—dressed in blue jeans, a blue-and-white-striped sweater, a jacket, and a wool cap—strolled into the Jefferson Federal Savings and Loan on Fifth Avenue and shoved a .38-caliber revolver directly into bank teller Shannon Hill's face.

"Money," he whispered. "Now."

Hill was struggling with the safe when branch manager Jill Tapscott stumbled onto the scene.

Anderson redirected his gun.

"You. Over here with her."

The tellers handed over $1,000 in cash, though Anderson replied, "That's not enough."

For the next few minutes, Tapscott stood within arm's length of Anderson's revolver, watching helplessly as her employee emptied her drawer. Hill handed over rolls of change, $150 in marked bills, as well as over $13,000 in traveler's checks. Forced to stare down the same barrel, Jane Baird, another employee, offered the cash from her drawer as well. Tapscott handed over traveler's checks in an attempt to appease him. Anderson slipped the checks and cash into a yellow bag and left without firing a shot.

The bank employees estimated that Anderson exited the bank approximately six minutes after entering. He left on foot, converging with the other pedestrians on the busy city street.

Officer Frank Erwin was the first to arrive on the scene. After taking Tapscott's description of the robber, he immediately spread word across police radios—they were looking for a stocky black male about six feet tall wearing a three-quarter-length brown coat and a matching colored hat.

At 3:55 p.m., Officer Charles Newfield—who had been working a shift at a nearby Sears department store—stepped outside to observe a man who matched the description. Officer Newfield watched as the suspect turned onto Second Alley, and while he started after him, brushing past people on the sidewalk, he soon lost visual contact.

However, the gunshots that erupted just moments later quickly put him back on the trail.

A few blocks away, Officer R. E. Middleton, a plainclothes police officer, spotted Anderson and shouted, "Halt! Police!" to no avail. Anderson sprinted toward the Southern Motor Inn Motel, his yellow bag swinging behind him, and upon reaching for his gun, Middleton and his partner opened fire. Anderson returned fire, and after spotting the squad car squealing to a halt just before him, he fired again. The officers in the squad car traded shots as well, downing Anderson directly beside the motel pool, his pockets overflowing with rolls of coins and traveler's checks, his yellow bag crumpled beside him.

The Birmingham Police had apprehended their suspect with swift efficiency.

It would have been deemed good police work, if it weren't for the officer who lost his life in the process.

Always a team player, Sergeant Albert Eugene Ballard ("Gene" to his friends) agreed to take the temporary position as patrol sergeant to help offset the number of patrolmen who had been transferred to work the anticrime task force. Trading in his administrative position for police cruiser 117, Gene had begun patrolling the downtown beat earlier that day. A husband and father of two, Gene was known around the force as being trustworthy and dependable. Police Chief Bill R. Myers called Gene "one of the finest police officers we have" and a "morally good man."

Just minutes after leaving the bank, Josephus Anderson spotted Sergeant Ballard's police car on the 200 block of 19th Street. Ballard called to him, motioning him over, and the man carrying the yellow bag obediently leaned into the patrol car as if to engage in friendly conversation.

Ballard opened his mouth to speak when Anderson pulled his gun, firing three times into Ballard's chest at point-blank range.

Josephus Anderson was no stranger to the law.

At nineteen, he was first arrested for defrauding a hotel, and in the eighteen years leading up to the Birmingham bank robbery, he'd racked up an additional dozen convictions in various states. At the time of the shooting, there were warrants for his arrest for charges ranging from grand larceny to auto theft. Anderson had a habit of getting arrested, making parole, and drifting to new locations where people wouldn't recognize him. In the early 1960s, he received five years for armed robbery in Milwaukee, though he was released early before being arrested yet again for the very same crime in 1968. He was found not guilty of bank robbery in 1974, though he was convicted again in 1977, where he served two years of an eight-year sentence before his release from the Federal Correctional Institution in Terre Haute, Indiana, on September 16, 1979. He headed south—most likely acquiring a gun in Atlanta—before continuing on to Birmingham, despite the unseasonably cold November chill.

Birmingham Police Chief Bill Myers was at a loss for words upon hearing the news of Ballard's death.

"How many times have we said if we're going to cut down on crime we have to keep the habitual offender off the street . . . The entire criminal justice system must bear responsibility. This individual's record bears that out."

Deputy Chief Tommy Rouse agreed, adding, "Virtually all [Anderson's] adult life has been spent in correctional institutions and he hasn't been corrected."

Birmingham police worked round the clock in an attempt to pin their cop killer.

Detectives Hurst and Grubbs worked overtime, painting a violent history of their suspect—the man shot by the motel pool. Not only had Anderson been found with the marked bank bills, but also, two ballistics experts agreed that the "bullets found in Sergeant Ballard's body and his car were fired from the pistol taken from the appellant."

Yet while Birmingham police had the suspect's fingerprints, they couldn't uncover his name.

Meanwhile, the Chicago police (who were also searching for Anderson) found themselves in the opposite situation—a name with no prints. As Detective Hurst later explained, "They had the name and wanted the prints, and we had the prints and wanted the name."

But managing workable prints out of Anderson was no easy task.

The *Birmingham News* reported that the Chicago Police Department had previously had a difficult time obtaining his fingerprints, most likely because Anderson had either developed a technique to ensure inaccurate printing or because of an oil-like secretion on his skin.

Regardless, eventually, their work paid off and the Birmingham police tracked his name from Chicago.

On Friday, December 7, just a little over a week after Sergeant Gene Ballard's murder, three detectives, a deputy district attorney, a sheriff's deputy, a nurse, and the chief of police, among others, crowded into the small room in Cooper Green Hospital where Anderson lay. Anderson had been shot twice by police—once in the abdomen and once in the mouth—warranting a brace around his jaw.

"Josephus Anderson?" the deputy asked, reading the indictment.

The room turned silent as law enforcement awaited an answer.

"Is that your name?" the deputy continued.

"My name is Robert," Anderson croaked.

"All right, Josephus R. Anderson," the deputy agreed, glancing down at his papers. "I have warrants here, one for assaulting a police officer with a deadly weapon, make that two assaulting a police officer with a deadly weapon, robbery, and a murder."

Anderson stayed silent, remaining that way until the officers left him there to stare at his untouched food tray.

When asked about his impressions of the suspect, Police Chief Myers said, "It would be difficult for me to express my thoughts because it might prejudice the case—I obviously have particularly strong feelings about this case."

Myers managed to bite his tongue, though others wouldn't.

Excessive news coverage of Sergeant Ballard's death allowed nearly every Birmingham citizen to become fully aware of the grisly details, making a fair and just trial virtually impossible within the city.

Anderson's hearing was eventually moved four hours south to Mobile, Alabama, where it was believed justice could more easily prevail.

Two years after Ballard's death, on the night Josephus Anderson's case was deemed a mistrial in a Mobile courtroom, nineteen-year-old Michael Donald watched his home team, the University of South Alabama Jaguars, lose to the Tulsa Hurricanes after coming back from a six-point deficit in the final thirty seconds of the basketball game. Disappointed, he left his sister Betty's TV room a few minutes later, wandering into the living room, where other family members were gathered playing a game of cards. Cards were dealt, and Michael's niece Vanessa handed him a dollar, asking him to buy her a pack of cigarettes at the nearby Gulf station. He agreed and started toward the door.

No one expected it to be the last time they saw Michael breathing.

FOURTH LOOP
A FLOWER IN THE FOREST

Birmingham, November 29–December 4, 1979

Oh, God, I need help . . .

In the days following Sergeant Gene Ballard's death, the Birmingham Police Department honored his memory by displaying black armbands and patches on their uniforms.

On Tuesday, December 4, Police Chief Myers sent an interoffice memo that read simply: "Sergeant Gene Ballard was fatally wounded on Nov. 29, 1979 while driving police car 117. In his honor the number 117 will be retired effective immediately. This number will no longer be utilized to designate any police unit within the Police Department."

The police wanted nothing more than a speedy prosecution, and while it appeared like an open and shut case, information remained spotty. Much of this was to blame on witnesses' unwillingness to come forward. Gene Ballard was fatally wounded between 3:35 and 4:00 p.m. on a crowded city street in downtown Birmingham, yet the police officers arrived on the scene to find—quite frustratingly—that not a single person could so much as point in the direction the assailant had fled.

During a joint press conference with Birmingham Mayor Richard Arrington the following day, Police Chief Myers made his frustration public.

"Something has been reported to me that is very shocking—people at the scene refusing to cooperate with police."

"It's completely disgusting to me after hearing all these remarks about law and order that so many people would refuse to cooperate when a police officer is murdered . . . It seems to me many of the people in the area were more concerned about a little traffic jam than they were with apprehending the murderer of Sgt. Ballard. There were hundreds of people in the area where the crime occurred, and the greatest portion of them ran or refused to cooperate . . . If the public is going to demand that the police do something about crime in this city, then I'm going to demand that the public do its part. And right now they are not."

Out of those hundreds of witnesses, only ten initially came forward.

By the following Monday, an additional six slunk into police headquarters to make statements. Myers grumbled that while police officers were working the crime scene, several citizens went so far as to curse the officers for interrupting their daily routine.

Myers chalked up the lack of witnesses to sheer cowardice, a "lack of guts," and stressed civic responsibility.

"It's about time we insist the public become more cooperative and accept their responsibility," Myers said.

For Birmingham, like Tuscaloosa years before, it was time to accept the challenge.

Kathy Sutton remembers all too well the day Josephus Anderson shot and killed her father. She was twenty-five at the time and had just come home from work, returning to her Alberta City home.

The doorbell rang, an unexpected visitor.

"My aunt came over to tell me," she recounted. "But most people found out from the TV."

Upon hearing that her father had been shot, Kathy jumped in the car and made the hour-long trek to the Birmingham home of her step-mother, Kalliopi. There, she was abruptly introduced to the unwanted stardom thrust upon her.

"When my father was killed, the media would call our house to talk to somebody, they would be outside in the street . . . It was really hard to grieve because they were in your face. They were ugly, like, 'You're not going to talk to us?' It was really hard because it takes a while to process all that."

This experience further solidified Sutton's distrust in others, the media, in particular.

"People are so . . . judgmental. Dad would tell me don't believe everything you read or see on TV. And to this day, I go by that because he was right. People—and reporters especially—can just be so blood-thirsty for a story."

Kalliopi Hartley, Gene's second wife and Kathy's stepmother, re-members that day as well.

"The last time I saw him was around 9:00 or 9:30," she explained. "I'd made breakfast and he'd eaten, gotten dressed, walked to the door. I'd come down with a bladder infection a few days before, so he'd call me a few times during the day to check on me. But he always did, three or four times a day. He called me around 2:00 p.m. that day, and I told him I'd gotten some medication, and I said thanks for checking on me and that was it. Whenever we hung up we always told each other we loved each other, and those were the last words he ever told me."

Just a few hours later, she, too, received an unexpected knock on her door.

She had been crocheting an afghan at the kitchen table, occasion-ally glancing up at the television set as her fingers worked the needle. The clock read 4:15 p.m.

"Then I heard the knock and it was our pastor's wife telling me that

Gene had been hurt. She didn't know anything else and Gene always told me, if anything happened to him, just to stay put and they'd send someone for me. I called the police department to see if they'd heard anything, but of course they lied to me and said no. I asked if they were sending someone for me and they said yes."

Kalliopi dressed, grabbed her purse, then waited dutifully on her front porch for the police car to arrive and take her to her husband.

"And I'm standing on the front porch when I see the guy in charge of the chaplain program and one of Gene's best friends, Bobby Lamb, walking up. And they have big smiles on their faces. I just started screaming because I knew what that meant. Nobody was saying, 'Hurry, come on, time to go downtown and see Gene.' They were just grinning like they knew he was with the Lord."

The police chaplain walked Kalliopi back into her living room, sat her down in her chair, and started praying.

"I just felt very calm and peaceful," Kalliopi recalled, "and I knew everything was going to be okay and that God would protect us."

Soon after, Police Chief Myers paid a visit to the home as well, and Kalliopi distinctly recalled gripping Myers's hands and informing him that she wholeheartedly forgave the man who shot her husband because God had forgiven her sins as well.

"And in God's eyes," she continued slowly, "there's no sin any bigger than any other. Whether you tell a lie or kill somebody, it's all the same in God's eyes."

Sergeant Albert Eugene Ballard was pronounced dead a few minutes past four on Thursday, November 29, 1979, though the funeral wouldn't occur until the following Monday.

While they originally planned for a Saturday funeral, Sutton recalled that she and her stepmother felt great pressure from the Birmingham

Police Department to postpone the funeral until after the Alabama-Auburn football game owing to the number of officers required to work that day.

The family agreed to postpone until after the game to ensure that all the officers could properly pay their respects.

The Crimson Tide was undefeated going into the Iron Bowl on Saturday, December 1, 1979. They were defending their previous year's national championship title, though on that blustery December afternoon, they found themselves playing more like the underdogs than the champions. They tried desperately to piece together a third quarter rally against rival Auburn, but four Alabama fumbles in that quarter alone seemed like certain defeat. Against all odds, Steadman Shealy's stunning touchdown in the fourth quarter gave Bama the win.

The sports section of the *Birmingham News* reported: "Always Bible-quoting Shealy could paraphrase an Old Testament dictum describing what happened on a cloudless, cold Iron Bowl Day: 'Alabama giveth, Alabama taketh away.'"

Forty-eight hours prior to her father's funeral, Kathy Sutton understood the poignancy of that quote far better than most.

Three hundred police cars arrived for the funeral procession, including cars from throughout the state, some even making the two-and-a-half-hour drive from Columbus, Georgia. The procession wove through downtown Birmingham, and behind the patrol cars, motorcycles, and honor guard, walked Birmingham Mayor Richard Arrington, as well as Police Chief Myers, among other local dignitaries.

The march ended at the back steps of City Hall, where Charles Smith, a fingerprint technician, played a haunting rendition of "Flowers of the Forest," a Scottish lament for fallen warriors.

The funeral that followed was more than a bit unorthodox.

For one, rather than calling it a funeral, Kalliopi insisted it be called a "victory ceremony." The Reverend Bobby Britt presided, quoting Kalliopi as saying, "Many people might not understand what [victory ceremony] means, but they will before they leave."

Following the eulogy by Bob Fields, founder of the Fellowship of Christian Law Enforcement, Reverend Bobby Britt walked to the stage, making it known to all who were present that Ballard's service as a police officer was "only a way to put food on the table, to pay utility bills . . . so he could spend his other time spreading the Word."

The reverend continued: "I've never done this at a funeral, but I'm going to give you a chance to know Gene's Savior."

Then, he asked the people in the audience to walk to the front and publicly commit themselves to Christ.

The choir sang as people began "to trickle out of the pews, most of them middle-aged policemen, some with their wives." Police chaplains surrounding the casket met the newly committed with open arms. The casket was suddenly inundated with both flowers and believers, sparking an indescribably powerful scene, according to Kalliopi.

"Our church held about 750 people," Kalliopi, noted. "But on the day of Gene's funeral, there were close to 2,500."

"The love that poured out for Gene," she had stated in the *Birmingham News* thirty years prior, "was just magnified by those who came forward for the Lord."

Yet daughter Kathy recalled how viewing her father in the casket hadn't afforded her the same closure.

"This is the weirdest thing," she began, "and my mother [Ballard's first wife] had an experience similar to this. Dad must've been in horrible pain because when I saw him in the coffin it . . . didn't look like my father. For years I would have dreams that he wasn't really dead. It just didn't look like him. I'd seen my grandmother in a coffin and she looked like she was sleeping, but this didn't look like my father."

Compounding this lack of closure was that by the December third funeral, Ballard's killer had yet to be formally charged. This wouldn't occur until the following Friday, four days later, as the police officers entered his room at Cooper Green Hospital.

However, one positive result of Ballard's funeral was a renewed sense of unity among Birmingham's citizens. Mark Winne reported that white police officer George Sands, who, just the previous summer, nearly lost his job for mistakenly shooting African-American Bonita Carter, marched alongside African-American Reverend Abraham Woods, who had previously called for Sands's removal. Yet both men put their squabbles aside in order to honor the memory of a police officer they both greatly admired. Earlier in the day, Mayor Arrington had spotted Sands and Woods walking alongside one another in the parade, noting that unity "may be Sgt. Ballard's legacy."

Measuring in at nearly six feet tall and two hundred pounds, Gene Ballard was a man to be reckoned with. His daughter made note of his "imposing figure," recalling how dates would stop by her house to pick her up, only to step inside the front door to find her police officer father displaying all his typical accoutrement: gun, nightstick, handcuffs.

"I don't think he was trying to scare them to death," she laughed. "It's just what he had on when he got home."

Josephus Anderson never knew Gene for the football-loving father he was. Nor was he aware of Gene's predilection for *Jeopardy!*, his love for golf, or that he had recently been named a police chaplain. Anderson knew nothing of Gene's childhood on a farm just outside of Gordo, where he and four brothers and three sisters—along with their parents—maintained a 223-acre farm. He knew nothing of the good or bad of Gene Ballard—his loyalty or his quick temper.

Kalliopi Hartley, Gene's second wife, understood the depths of his loyalty, marrying on June 22, 1969, just weeks before the first troops were withdrawn from Vietnam, a month before man first walked on the moon.

"I can't remember if it was our first anniversary or our second," Kalliopi recalled, "but I was working that day and Gene had the day off. And when I walked in the door, he had the song . . . I think it was Ray Price . . . the song 'Sweetheart of the Year' playing on the stereo. And he had the table set, dinner prepared. It was just really special. He was always doing that kind of thing."

"And another thing we always did," she continued, "we never took our rings off. If he had to have surgery or something, I took his wedding ring off and put it back on afterward. The same for me. The only time it was taken off by somebody other than me was when he passed, when the coroner took it off. But when we were getting ready for the funeral, I slipped the ring right back on his finger at the funeral home one last time. And he was buried with it."

Yet Josephus Anderson considered none of this as he pulled the trigger.

He simply viewed Sergeant Gene Ballard as an obstacle between him and his freedom, and so he aimed and fired, hardly skipping a beat.

One November afternoon, as Kalliopi crocheted an afghan at her kitchen table, as Kathy drove home from work, Josephus Anderson raised his .38 caliber revolver and shot the husband and father three times in the chest before falling himself just minutes later, by a motel swimming pool.

Sergeant Gene Ballard didn't die immediately.

If the bank tellers' timeline is accurate, then we know that Anderson left the bank at approximately 3:34 p.m. and Gene's last radio cry for help occurred at 3:49 p.m. It's possible Gene lived for nearly fifteen to twenty additional minutes before University Hospital pronounced him dead at a few minutes after 4:00.

Around 4:00 p.m., as Gene struggled for his life, Anderson bled as well, at the Southern Motor Inn just a few blocks away.

Gasping, Gene's voice blasted across police radios one last time before signing off.

"Oh, God, I need help—200 block of 19th Street . . ."

The impact of the bullets had forced Gene's foot into the accelerator, propelling his car forward into a utility pole, crumpling the hood.

While most of the witnesses fled, Sandra Parker, a nurse who happened to be passing by, ran to assist the wounded officer. Though her efforts were ultimately unsuccessful, Police Chief Myers was moved by her selfless act, offering her a commendation for her bravery.

"I'm just really touched by it," Parker said. "I think it's really nice of them to give this much recognition for something I thought was a citizen's duty to do."

In the past, Myers probably would have agreed, though after witnessing such a "disgusting lack of guts" by the other citizens who chose to flee the scene, Parker's ability to fulfill her civic duty seemed all the more commendable.

The story of Sergeant Gene Ballard's death isn't simply the tale of a police officer who fell in the line of duty. Instead, it's the story of a *white* police officer who fell due to three shots fired at close range by a *black* assailant. Neither man intended for their ill-fated interaction to strike such a racial chord, yet the circumstances made it inevitable. Birmingham was only a few decades removed from Bull Connor's violent reign as commissioner of public safety, and black and white citizens alike remembered the police dogs straining on their leashes and the fire hoses spraying civil rights protestors to the ground. In the mid-sixties, Birmingham had earned the nickname "Bombingham" because of the many bombs set off in the black districts of the city, and this history, coupled with a more recent incident involving a white police officer killing an innocent black woman just months before, caused the Ballard murder to be the final ingredient in a perfect storm that had been brewing for decades.

On November 29, 1979, Josephus Anderson, who happened to be black, walked into the Jefferson Federal Savings and Loan and demanded money. Minutes later, Sergeant Gene Ballard, who happened to be white, called the suspect over to his car.

Gene was simply in the wrong place.

Anderson was simply in the wrong place.

The intersecting forces that collided to bring them together at the 200 block of 19th Street were not the result of generations of racial violence or any personal ill will toward one another. Anderson fired because Gene was there, though the racial overtones that ultimately seeped into the courtroom only allowed for the violence to ripple out further.

Gene Ballard, a veteran police officer, had served under the infamous Commissioner of Public Safety Eugene "Bull" Connor, who is most remembered for encouraging violent tactics such as high-powered water hoses and police dogs against Birmingham's black civil rights protesters. Despite enduring a barrage of rocks and bottles thrown his way, Gene survived the riots unscathed, and as his daughter noted, managed to "put all racial issues behind him."

She recounted a particular story in which her father—who had a rare blood type—received a call from the Red Cross informing him that a pair of newborn twins was in desperate need of his blood. Kathy recalled her father dressing and rummaging in his pockets for his car keys.

"Where are you going?" she asked.

"Red Cross," he replied, stepping out the door. "There are two little black babies who need my blood or they'll die."

This is not to imply that Gene wasn't deeply affected by the race riots—many police officers were—but Kathy recalled her father explaining it to her in terms she could understand.

"You know, Kathy," he began, "there are bad policemen just like there are bad everything. Not everything is good in every situation."

"What's sad," he continued, "is that there are some people without a conscience. You won't understand this because you have one. But I've seen kids who are whipped, not because they stole but because they were *caught* stealing. See the difference?"

She did.

It was a lesson she never forgot.

It's so commonplace it's almost become a cliché: the police officer who, just days before his retirement, dies while working his final beat. Yet Sergeant Gene Ballard's death reminds us that clichés are often rooted in truth.

Gene was, in fact, eligible for retirement the following Saturday, just two days after his murder.

Not that he had any intention of retiring.

Most likely, he intended to celebrate his twentieth anniversary on the force by watching the Iron Bowl along with the rest of the state.

On December 4, 1979, the day following the funeral, Police Chief Myers remarked, "One thing I hope the community realizes from the tragic death of Sgt. Ballard is that a real danger exists on the street for police officers. Officers do have to make life or death decisions. If they make the wrong decision, sometimes it can cost the officer his life."

Most likely the "wrong decision" that Myers was referring to was the fact that Ballard's revolver remained in his holster throughout his interaction with Anderson.

"I really had a lot of confidence in him," Kathy recalled. "He was above average intelligence. He was a good shot. I think . . . I just don't think he thought."

Jane Tidwell, the Ballards' neighbor, worked at the Jefferson Federal Savings and Loan and was present on the day Anderson walked in wielding his gun.

"And . . . she came to the house later that day," Kathy explained, "and I heard her talking to my stepmother about how upset she was that my dad was shot . . . he had lived through so much. But there was a reduction in force and he was put back on the street. Without a partner. I just don't think a policeman should ever be left alone."

The 1979 list of Alabama Peace Officers Killed in the Line of Duty alluded to the force reduction as well. When summarizing Gene's death, the final lines read:

"[Josephus Anderson] was charged with bank robbery and murder of a police officer."

And then, quite chillingly: "Ballard was alone."

Today, his grave marker sags in the dry grass atop a slight incline at Jefferson Memorial Cemetery, a few miles outside downtown Birmingham. It's a modest marker, the name BALLARD embossed in the center, a cross on one side, and a police badge indicating his work as a chaplain on the other. His marker overlooks a busy city street, as well as a strip mall overflowing with chain stores such as Super Target, Belk, and Best Buy, all clearly within view. Flowers line the graves, and groundskeepers continually buzz past on their carts, cleaning out the vases and replacing the dead flowers with fresh ones.

On the day I entered the cemetery, I spent ninety minutes attempting to locate Ballard's grave marker, returning to the funeral home twice for more specific directions. I was offered various highlighted maps indicating where Ballard was supposed to be buried, though his marker wasn't where the funeral home employees assured me it was. And so, after filing through the rows to no avail, I recruited a pair of groundskeepers for help, and they, too, began scouring the vast land alongside me, jabbing their shovels into the earth, noting how sometimes grave markers get swallowed up by grass and time without anyone ever noticing.

Eventually, we stumbled across the marker, only a hundred or so feet from where the map had indicated.

"Believe it or not, they can be tricky to keep track of sometimes," a groundskeeper admitted. "The grass just grows so fast . . . it makes it easy to forget."

As I pulled out of the cemetery moments later, I noticed a sign to my left: "Birmingham Police Department Firing Range And Training Facility." An arrow pointed to a small road adjacent to the property line of the cemetery.

As I drove past, I couldn't help but wonder with what regularity Ballard frequented that range, how often he passed the cemetery where he would one day rest.

"Once," Kathy Sutton explained, speaking slowly, "I saw Dad and my husband pick up a tree. Not just a log, but an actual tree. We were in Birmingham and this horrible tornado had come through, and . . . I saw him pick it up. And I thought, 'My God.'"

Kathy went on to describe the tree's hulk, how its great size and cumbersome shape made it virtually impossible to get a handle on it, how the tornado had ripped through the landscape, destroying everything in its path, regardless of anything but proximity.

How no roots wound deep enough to keep any tree upright.

How the tornado had caused the world to collapse all around her.

"And . . . and then I just saw Dad pick the tree up," she explained, baffled, "and I just couldn't believe he was that strong."

She paused before continuing.

"But, you know, he was," she whispered. "He really was. Believe it or not, my father was really that strong."

PART II The Last Lynching

FIFTH LOOP
A PACK OF CIGARETTES

Mobile, March 20–21, 1981

And that was the last time I saw him.

For Michael Donald, the morning of Friday, March 20, 1981, started out just like any other. Since December 1979—just a little over a week after Sergeant Gene Ballard was murdered—Michael had been working the night shift as a stuffer for the *Mobile Register,* clocking in for the last time on Wednesday evening at 9:00 p.m. and leaving around 4:30 a.m. the following morning.

That Friday Michael dedicated much of the afternoon to playing basketball at various nearby recreation centers. One of Michael's close friends recalled playing ball with him at the Busby Recreation Center on North Lawrence Street until close to 3:00 p.m., at which time his friend had to leave for work.

The friend—whose name has been omitted from the FBI files—noted that he and Michael always played on the same team and were never opponents. After the game the pair walked outside for a breather.

"Then I told Michael I had to go to work around 3:00 o'clock and I don't think Mike knew when I left because I left about ten minutes till

3:00 o'clock . . . and he was still playing ball," the friend recalled, "and that was the last time I saw him."

Another friend—one who, according to his statement, considered himself Michael's closest friend—confirmed playing basketball with Michael at the recreation center as late as 7:30 p.m. that night.

Another witness claimed he'd seen Michael at around 7:30 p.m. on Morgan Street, that he recalled his friend wearing trousers and a T-shirt, and that Michael had plans to go home and shower before heading over to his girlfriend's house.

Yet another disagreed, claiming Michael was wearing red jump shorts, a white shirt, and blue-and-white tennis shoes, and that he was actually standing outside of Busby Recreation Center.

Despite conflicting reports of his whereabouts, the many witnesses—along with various other friends and family members—all agreed on one point: Michael was a quiet young man.

The word "quiet" is repeated over and over again, both in firsthand interviews as well as in the FBI reports.

"Michael Donald kept to himself, was soft spoken and in fact spoke very little to anyone," explained a close friend. The friend went on to describe Michael as, "a clean-cut type" and not the type of person to wander the streets. Michael "did not like to roam," the friend added, and "stayed pretty much around his house." He was "not a night person and did not drink alcoholic beverages." However, this friend later admitted that Michael had been known to smoke cigarettes on occasion and even enjoyed a rare marijuana cigarette, usually following his paydays on Mondays.

According to Michael's mother, Beulah Mae Donald, the Donald family was close-knit, and although Michael was "very quiet," he was "very much a part of this close-knit family." Michael was frugal, and she told investigators that, to her knowledge, he did not smoke or drink. Later, she admitted to reporters that he did smoke, and though she'd warned him against it, he'd replied, "I'm going to college. Can't I have a cigarette?"

She claimed that Michael "centered his activities around her family," and while he occasionally borrowed small amounts of money on Friday nights, he'd always repay it by Monday after receiving his paycheck from the *Mobile Register*. He earned $124 a week, which may have contributed to his frugal nature.

After graduating from Murphy High School in 1980, Michael immediately began training as a brick mason at Carver Technical School in Mobile. Mrs. Donald described her son as "a slow talker who never had much to say," recalling that he'd told her he wasn't going into work that Friday night, and instead, was going to his sister Betty's to watch the University of South Alabama vs. Tulsa basketball game with various siblings and relatives.

One family member described Michael as "the sort of person who if he felt there was a difficulty on the street in front of him, he would cross the street and walk on the other side." The family member highly doubted that there was any likelihood that Michael would have entered a nearby nightclub to purchase cigarettes if the Gulf station was closed. He also explained that Michael and his girlfriend (whose existence is unconfirmed) were "having some difficulties lately" and "this was one of the reasons why he was not visiting with [name omitted] on that Friday night."

Bob Eddy, an investigator for the Mobile District Attorney's Office, concurred with these characterizations of Michael Donald, accurately recalling Michael's remarkably clean slate.

"He didn't have any enemies; no one who wanted to get even with him. It was nothing gang-related. Everyone who met him liked him. He was said to be a real good employee for the *Mobile Register*. And his family was just an excellent family, really good people, really fine people," Eddy confirmed.

"We could find nothing on Michael," agreed former Mobile police sergeant and current Andalusia police chief Wilbur Williams, one of the first officers to arrive on the murder scene that morning. "He'd never been arrested, never even had a ticket. It appeared that all he did was shoot baskets, work his job at the *Mobile Register*, and go home."

Yet he had a sense of humor as well, *Mobile Register* reporter Michael Wilson noting that he "made his oldest sister, Mary Jackson, laugh with his goofy version of James Brown's popcorn dance."

Sometime early on Friday evening—perhaps between basketball games at the recreation center—one of Michael's longtime childhood friends recalled letting Michael borrow a soft drink bottle to spare him having to pay the deposit. Allegedly, Michael returned the bottle to his friend at 7:15 p.m. before reemerging once more around 8:00 p.m. Spotting him, the friend noted how he and Michael had talked and wrestled some in the backyard. The friend reported that, "Donald stated he was going to a party, but he did not mention what kind of party nor where the party was to be."

However, an unnamed female friend of Michael's recalled spending time with him between 7:00 and 8:00 p.m. as well, slightly contradicting the timeline set by the friend who had allowed Michael to borrow the bottle. The female friend noted that she had known Michael for nearly two years and that they often played basketball together at Busby. She claimed that he rose to leave approximately an hour after arriving, but not before grabbing a comic book that he promised to read while watching the basketball game at his sister's house.

The party turned out to be a family gathering at his sister Betty Wyatt's home. Betty welcomed him into her Orange Grove unit on North Jackson Street near the State Docks. Michael was the youngest of eight, the baby of the family.

At 9:30 p.m., Michael wandered into the TV room, where he met with a few male family members and sat down to watch the second half of the South Alabama vs. Tulsa game. March Madness was in full swing, and the previous night, the Indiana Hoosiers had defeated the University of Alabama at Birmingham Blazers 72–56, while Wichita State had lost handily to LSU with the same score, knocking both teams from the tournament.

Certainly there were more high-profile games to watch that evening—the highly contested North Carolina vs. Kentucky matchup, as well as Virginia vs. BYU—though Michael preferred rooting for his home team: South Alabama in the NIT division. When Michael arrived at Betty's house at halftime, he was pleased to find his team holding its own, though the Jags' twenty-three turnovers played a pivotal role in their downfall.

After the Jags' heart-crushing 69–68 defeat, Michael excused himself from the room, explaining to his family that he was going for a pack of cigarettes.

This, too, however, is debatable.

While several FBI files report Michael left the house to buy *himself* a pack of cigarettes, others report that he was actually buying a pack for his niece, Vanessa.

Though redacted (like most names in the FBI files), two more of Michael's friends confirmed seeing him at precisely 11:05 p.m., as he stepped outside Betty Wyatt's housing unit on his way to purchase cigarettes. The statement recounted:

"As they were leaving their residence and going to their automobile, which was parked in front of their residence, Michael Donald walked out of the residence at [address omitted] and walked to the sidewalk which runs along Beauregard Street, and turned in a southwesterly direction, which would lead to the Gulf station located several blocks away. As he was leaving, [name omitted] exchanged greetings with Michael Donald but no conversation was held with him."

The second friend, who was also walking toward the automobile, noted that Michael walked along the "brick wall located on Beauregard Street . . . which eventually leads to the Gulf station located a block or so from that point."

No witnesses reported seeing Michael after 11:05 p.m. on Friday, March 20. The following day, police officers questioned the employees at the nearby Gulf station, as well as all other gas station attendants in the area, but no one had any recollection of the nineteen-year-old in the blue warm-up jacket, gray sweater, blue jeans, and leather belt with the Led Zeppelin buckle.

"That's because he wasn't at the Gulf station," explained Wilbur Williams, one of the lead investigators on the case and the current chief of police in nearby Andalusia. "The Gulf station was closed, so he was walking toward the 7-Eleven on the corner of Springhill and Kennedy."

By 1:00 a.m., Michael's mother, Beulah Mae, was growing concerned; it was not like Michael to stay out so late. She spent a mostly sleepless night waiting for the front door to squeak, announcing his arrival, though the house remained silent.

According to *New York Times* writer Jesse Kornbluth, Beulah Mae eventually dozed off, only to wake from a dream in which she saw a "steel-gray casket in her living room." Beulah Mae described the dream in detail, noting that every time she attempted to peer into the casket, a voice said, "You don't need to see this."

Wide awake by 2:00 a.m., she sat restlessly on her couch sipping coffee until dawn, at which point she made her way into the yard to begin raking. As she collected the leaves, a woman delivering insurance policies spotted Mrs. Donald and casually informed her that a body had been discovered.

Nearby, on the corner of Dauphin Street and Georgia Avenue, an elderly man named Joe Buck began sifting through the Dauphin Way Baptist Church Dumpster to collect cardboard for a friend. As he reached into the bin, his hand grazed a black trifold wallet. The man leafed through it, noting Michael Donald's Carver Technical identification card, Medicaid card, a picture, a condom, a home telephone number, and entirely void of money.

Though the time frame differs, according to Beulah Mae, at around 10:00 a.m. her phone rang, an elderly woman (Buck's landlord) on the other end.

It was then that Mrs. Beulah Mae Donald heard the chilling words that haunted her the rest of her life: Michael's wallet had been plucked from a Dumpster behind a church not far from their home.

At first, Beulah Mae read it as a good sign, proof that he was alive.

"No, baby," whispered the woman on the other end, "they killed your son. You'd better send somebody over."

Re-creating the timeline of the evening of March 20 and the early morning of March 21 is far more difficult than one might expect. So many witness statements contradict one another, rendering a full and accurate re-creation of that night virtually impossible. Every detail is called into question, doubted, unverifiable.

This lack of agreement was particularly apparent between the Mobile Police Department and the Donald family, and was perhaps emblematic of a greater problem: a perceived communication breakdown that eventually caused the Donald family to question the sincerity of the Mobile Police Department's efforts.

However, the FBI files confirmed what the Mobile Police Department had pieced together—that Michael *had* spent much of Friday afternoon playing basketball at Busby Recreation Center, and that he may have moved to nearby Springhill Recreation Center, where he played as late as 7:30 p.m.

However, it's even more difficult to track exactly what occurred between 8:00 and 9:30 p.m.

According to the FBI report, Michael and an unnamed female spent nearly an hour at the female's mother's house, at which point Michael borrowed the comic book and continued on his way. At 8:45, his un-named closest friend claimed Michael stopped by his house as well, though he hadn't been there to meet him. Various witnesses confirmed that by 9:30—halftime of the University of South Alabama vs. Tulsa game—a freshly showered Michael entered his sister Betty Wyatt's home and began watching television with family members. He stayed in Betty's home for the next ninety minutes before leaving one final time, for the cigarettes.

While sifting through the various versions of what occurred that night, the witness statements not only contradicted timelines, but Michael Donald's character as well. Some alleged acquaintances argued that Michael was not the basketball-loving, quiet young man prone to crossing the street when he smelled trouble. According to a few marginal, unsubstantiated witness statements Michael Donald was actually a drug-addled, homosexual hustler, as well as a dealer who regularly frequented prostitutes.

One prostitute claimed she met Michael on the corner of St. Francis and Hamilton, brought him home and had sex with him. She knew he often rode a bike, claiming that he'd parked it out back and that someone had stolen it on the night of their rendezvous.

"Did it appear as if this was his first time in, you know, the situation that he was in?" a detective later questioned the prostitute.

"No, it wasn't . . . he was well experienced," she replied.

However, portraying Michael as a pimp or a frequenter of prostitutes are both difficult stories to swallow, particularly because Michael often worked nights at the *Mobile Register*, a more than sufficient alibi.

Yet the prostitute wasn't alone in her less-than-flattering assessment of Michael Donald.

A male witness claimed that Michael had sold him "sets" of "T's and Blues" (pentazocine and tripelennamine) on numerous occasions.

The witness went on to explain that "Michael Donald and [name omitted] used to do sets together around the Flame Club and other clubs, and that they would beat the people for the money."

The witness claimed that Michael had been selling "sets" for a year, and often hung out on Herndon Avenue, chatting up white girls. The witness assured the detective that Michael "definitely sold drugs" but was "definitely not homosexual."

Police Chief Wilbur Williams recalled how these unsubstantiated claims proved detrimental to the case.

"One day we had three black transvestites come forth with information that Michael Donald was living a double life," Williams began.

They told us a story diametrically opposed to the other stories we'd been hearing about Michael Donald's character. They started talking about this double life he'd been living, that they'd had sex with him, that he was known to solicit favors on the street, that he was a big dope smoker. So what do we do as investigators? We can't afford not to find out the truth, so we start asking those kinds of questions to the family, and the family turns on us almost instantly. In their eyes, we weren't the ones out there trying to find out who killed their loved one, we were the bad people. It was becoming a full-fledged, unadulterated racial situation. We had no choice; we had to run these things to get to the bottom of it, but by asking the questions our relationship with the Donald family changed.

But despite the investigation that followed, no traces of drugs were ever found in Michael's bedroom or body.

Of the multitude of contradictory statements related to Michael's character, the vast majority concurred with the former: that Michael was quiet, considerate, a man without enemies. Nevertheless, an admitted prostitute, drug user, and a trio of transvestites depicted Michael as a hustler, a dealer, and a user, though their voices were certainly in the minority and were ultimately disproven.

"Turned out that was all a bunch of bull," explained Police Chief Wilbur Williams. "But at that point in time, we couldn't afford to ignore them. It was one of those 'damned if you do, damned if you don't' situations. What if he had lived a double life and we'd ignored it? Then we'd be damned. But because we began asking those incendiary questions to his family members we were still damned. But we had to run it to ground. We had to investigate every lead. It was our job."

The question of "Who was Michael Donald?" is far more complex than any individual assessment. Yet even when all the witness statements are taken together, we are still at a loss.

Despite any amount of research, there are still details we can never uncover, depths we have no way of reaching.

On Saturday, March 21, 1981, family members gathered together to await the news.

Nearly thirty years have passed since that day, and with them, much of the collective memory of Michael Donald.

News of Michael's death spread quickly. Everyone had a story to share, which only managed to muddle the case further.

In a newspaper article written shortly after his death, Michael's older sister Cecelia Perry stated, "When Michael wanted to go get some cigarettes at the Gulf Service Station we told him to ride his nephew's bike. It seemed funny to us because he insisted he would rather walk."

Yet walking fit well within Michael's routine.

"You heard the sound of a bouncing basketball before you saw him coming," *Mobile Register* reporter Michael Wilson noted. "He walked everywhere."

"We think he was just in the wrong place at the wrong time," Michael's sister Cecelia explained, echoing an assessment quite similar to those in both the Maddox and Ballard cases.

But nearly two years would pass before the police uncovered the true motive for Michael Donald's death, eerily close to Ms. Perry's initial assessment.

True, Michael *had* been in the wrong place at the wrong time.

But he also had the wrong skin color.

The following Saturday, March 28, nearly two thousand people crowded into the stifling hot Revelation Baptist Church where Dr. Leon Taylor preached for peace.

"We are hurting," he began, "but one wrong has already been done and another won't help."

He prayed that the Donald family would allow their fury to subside, that they would allow "God to work it out."

In attendance were various local black leaders, including NAACP presidents from as far as Florida and Georgia. In many ways it was similar to Sergeant Ballard's funeral—thousands packed into a church, dignitaries arriving from all regions of the South.

And there was something else they shared as well.

Taking a cue from Mamie Till-Mobley, mother of Emmett Till—a fourteen-year-old boy who was gruesomely murdered and tossed in the Tallahatchie River in 1955—Beulah Mae Donald decided on an open casket, as did the Ballard family.

"I wanted the world to see what they did to my baby," Mamie Till-Mobley had famously explained twenty-six years earlier.

And though it pained her immensely, Beulah Mae Donald did the same—keeping the casket door flung wide and allowing the world to peer in.

SIXTH LOOP
A DOMESTIC DISTURBANCE

Mobile, March 20–21, 1981

There was about nine of us out there.

In the early morning hours of Saturday, March 21, 1981, the police were called to Herndon Avenue, though not for Michael Donald.

At around 2:00 a.m., twenty-three-year-old Ralph Hayes was involved in a domestic disturbance with his girlfriend, Linda Odom, on nearby Dauphin Street. Linda had tried unsuccessfully to reach Ralph all night after he finished his shift as a pulpwood worker, but after listening to the phone ring one too many times, she decided she'd had enough. She gathered some belongings—including Ralph's stereo and television—and left Ralph's apartment on Herndon Avenue and made her way to a friend's house on nearby Dauphin Street.

"I guess she was mad at me for being so late coming home," Ralph later confessed. "Somebody had told her that I had gone out after I got off from work and had spent all of my money and had got drunk. I didn't even get paid."

Dressed in black corduroys, a beige shirt, and a blue jean hat, the white Cajun hailed a cab to drive him to Herndon Avenue. Upon arriving there, he instructed the cab driver to wait outside his apartment while he slipped inside to retrieve the fare. But rather than give the address to his own apartment, he had the cabbie park in front of a nearby apartment while he snuck in the back entrance to his own, stiffing the driver. He entered the empty apartment to find his girlfriend Linda missing, along with his TV and stereo.

A witness—Linda's friend—recalled hearing a knock on the Dauphin Street apartment door later that evening.

Linda's friend reached for the door handle as Ralph barged into the apartment, shouting for his girlfriend. Linda's friend replied she didn't know where Odom was.

"Well, where is my stuff?"

She didn't answer.

"Bitch," Ralph shouted, "you know you know where they at!"

Linda Odom stepped out from her hiding place, and she and Ralph began arguing.

"They were cursing," the friend remembered, as Ralph stomped into the bedroom behind Linda.

An unnamed person was apparently in the bedroom with her, causing Ralph to shout, "What the hell are you doing here with [name omitted]? This makes the third time I have caught you in the bedroom with [name omitted]."

Moments later, either Linda or her male companion picked up a knife, to which Ralph replied, "If you are going to use that, go ahead and stab me instead of acting like you want to do something."

Ralph and Linda took their fight to the streets, Linda's friend describing how Ralph was "hitting her and tearing her clothes off." The friend followed close behind as Ralph and Linda tromped in the direction of the WBLX radio station, just a little over a block away.

It's at this point when the friend recalled noticing something seemingly insignificant, though eventually, it would prove critical to the

Michael Donald case—"this black car in the back of the apartments and these two white guys [coming] from somewhere."

She paid little attention to it at the time, and instead, watched in horror as Ralph Hayes and Linda began slapping and kicking one another, eventually storming off in opposite directions.

According to the police statement, at 2:32 a.m., a police officer received a call of a disturbance and discovered Linda and her friend in the parking lot of the WBLX radio station, just down the street from both apartments. After being reassured that the dispute between Linda and Ralph had subsided, the officer drove down Herndon Avenue to investigate yet another noise complaint.

Twenty-six-year-old Henry Hays, who had allegedly been playing Spades with friends throughout the evening, was engaged in a domestic dispute of his own with a female from across the street. At the same time, a call was made to police regarding the cab driver still parked outside of what was believed to be Ralph Hayes's apartment. Three officers responded to the various calls, and Henry Hays stepped outside to chat with them. Meanwhile, one of the officers knocked on the cab window, waking the driver, and when asked why he was parked there, the man explained that a five-foot-eight, 150-pound shaggy-haired man who "gave the appearance of a gypsy" had stiffed him on his fare and that he had drifted off while waiting for his money. Henry Hays—whose father, Bennie Jack Hays, owned many of the rental properties on Herndon Avenue—agreed to assist the cab driver in tracking down the culprit, and the police officers left the pair to begin knocking on doors, unsuccessfully attempting to locate the man who had stiffed the cabbie.

But by this point, Ralph Hayes—the "shaggy-haired" cab stiffer in question—had already disappeared. According to former Mobile police sergeant and current Andalusia police chief Wilbur Williams, Ralph and his friend Jimmy Edgar returned to Herndon to pack a few things before asking Jimmy's brother Johnny to pick them up. Soon after,

Johnny, a cowboy hat atop his head, pulled up in his green Ford Torino, and the trio left just before daybreak.

Hours passed, tempers calmed, and eventually, Ralph Hayes, Linda Odom, and the others all stumbled off to separate bedrooms.

At around 5:30 a.m., a man on his way to work spotted a black male hanging in a vacant lot on Herndon Avenue, so the man flagged down a police officer to report it. Upon arriving at the scene, the officer discovered Michael's body in the camphor tree, just as it had been described to him.

Yet Police Chief Wilbur Williams remembered the morning slightly differently from how the FBI described it.

It was a beautiful morning in Mobile. Bright blue skies, no clouds, cool temperatures, probably in the fifties. That morning, there had been two calls to the Mobile Police Department almost simultaneously. One started out as a suspicious circumstance. An elderly gentlemen [Glen Harold Davis, sixty-one] who lived on Herndon Avenue, had a serious heart condition and his daily routine involved walking up Herndon Avenue to Springhill, turning west on Springhill, and just a short distance up was a bus bench, where he would catch his breath. He'd then walk on to a Winn Dixie, buy a morning newspaper, and reverse his tracks. Being the first day of spring, the equinox, it was still dark, but as he exited his residence, he saw someone standing on the sidewalk on his side of the street. Being a frail elderly man, Davis crossed to the other side of the street to get his paper. But when he returned, he saw the same man still loitering there, so he called the police, and said, in his words, that there was a "suspicious black male hanging around on Herndon Avenue." Minutes later, a stevedore drove by toward the state docks and saw a body there, so he used a pay phone and called the police. Two separate officers arrived from two separate calls. And they arrived to find probably the ghastliest scene they'd ever seen in their lives.

Williams, who arrived on the scene moments later, is still haunted by the grotesque manner in which Michael's body was hung—arm extended, rigor mortis already set in.

"Rigor mortis normally means a fairly significant amount of time has passed since the victim died," Williams explained. "But when you are involved in some kind of confrontation, the body produces a large amount of adrenaline—that fight or flight mentality—and the adrenaline in the muscle tissue will cause the muscle tissue to go into rigor mortis much faster than if the body was relaxed. And that's what happened to Michael."

After county coroner Dr. LeRoy Riddick visually observed the body at the crime scene, the police officers wrapped Michael Donald's body in a sheet and removed him from the tree. Sergeant Williams assisted in the process; his hands clasped Michael's body as they lowered him the few inches back to the ground.

"We did not untie the knot," Williams recalled. "We cut the knot. We knew we had to preserve it."

As the days passed, pressure to find Michael Donald's murderer continued to mount.

Wilbur Williams worked nonstop from early Saturday morning until Monday evening, dedicating much of that time to searching for the murder scene.

"Michael had a considerable amount of powdery, dusty type material on him," Williams remembered. "If you look at the pictures, you can see those areas on his blue jacket, his blue jeans. Judging by that and his injuries we knew that somewhere there was a hell of a crime scene. And if that crime scene could be located it would yield a mother lode of potential evidence."

In the days that followed, Mobile Police scoured the area.

"We spent several hours on our hands and knees searching for evidence," Williams recalled. "We went back to the Donald residence and determined within two or three minutes at what point he left."

The officers began retracing his steps, walking the various paths from Betty Wyatt's Orange Grove apartment to the gas station Michael never reached.

"Michael had a distance . . . probably as the crow would fly . . . half, maybe a sixth of a mile," Williams explained. "But the way you'd have to walk with blocks would be a little different."

Despite their efforts, Mobile Police would not uncover the scene of the murder until years later—a wooded area one mile north of the intersection of Highway 225 in nearby Baldwin County.

"All we found was one droplet of what appeared to be human blood on the sidewalk of the west side of Herndon Avenue," Williams recalled. "And Michael's body was on the east side."

But one drop of blood was not enough to convict anyone, particularly in the days prior to DNA analysis.

As the police attempted to assemble a case, Wilbur Williams was made aware of a piece of information that would initially prove quite valuable—that Herndon Avenue was a hotbed for Ku Klux Klan activity. The street was overflowing with Klansmen, including Henry Hays's father, Grand Titan Bennie Jack Hays, who owned various properties along the street.

"We got statements from all of them," Williams explained, "and then I looked at [a Klansman's] pickup truck kind of closely. I didn't search it, of course—I didn't have any warrant, and I didn't have any probable cause to get one—but right in front of a Ford Truck was a black Buick Wildcat with red interior, which was identified as belonging to Henry Hays. I walked by, kind of giving it a cursory look. If I had seen anything I could've gone further with it," he said regrettably, "but there was nothing there to see."

Tips began pouring in from all corners of the city, making it difficult for the Mobile Police to track down the sudden influx of leads.

However, one tip, the testimony of a cab patron named Johnny Ray Kelly, proved particularly interesting to Williams. "So early on March 21st, Johnny Ray Kelly stepped into my office and said, 'I was riding in a taxi cab with a friend of mine and we ran out of gas, and I was standing at the Freeman House, the coffee house, and all of the sudden, Ralph Hayes and Jimmy and Johnny Edgar walked up. Ralph Hayes was cleaning his fingers with a pocketknife. He had on a plaid flannel and a white t-shirt, and there was a spot of blood about as big as a softball. He was cleaning something out of his fingernails, I thought it was blood. I asked him what happened and he said 'We just hospital-whipped a nigger's ass.'"

Williams followed up on the lead, starting with Robert Davidson, the cab driver with whom Johnny Ray Kelly was supposedly riding.

"I located the cab driver, and I said, 'Robert, tell me about this Friday night and Saturday morning episode with Johnny Ray Kelly.' And Robert replied, 'Johnny said he had nothing better to do and wanted to ride with me, so we picked up a fare and took that fare to a club. I ran out of gas on the ride home. I coasted out and Johnny said, 'I'll sit here and wait,' and then he went to sleep."

Robert Davidson recounted how he snatched an empty plastic bottle from the back of a nearby pickup truck before walking to a nearby gas station, where he purchased seventy-five cents' worth of gas.

"Where was Johnny Kelly?" Williams asked Davidson.

"He was still asleep."

"Did you go to the Freeman House?"

"No."

"Did Johnny Kelly have a discussion with Ralph Hayes or Jimmy or Johnny?"

"Not that I know of."

Williams took his police work one step further, tracing Davidson to the gas station where he bought the bottle full of gas.

"It just so happened that that service station was one of the first to have video [surveillance], and it was about 2:45 a.m. when the cab driver bought the gas, and the clerk remembered the transaction. That location is almost five miles from the Freeman House, so that conversation between Ralph Hayes, the Edgar brothers, and Johnny Ray Kelly simply did not occur."

Nevertheless, on March 25—just four days after the murder—the Mobile Police Department's confidence in cab patron Johnny Ray Kelly's testimony led to the arrests of Ralph Hayes and brothers Jimmy and Johnny Edgar—three Cajuns whom Kelly had specifically named in his witness statement, as well as the men involved in the domestic disturbance with Linda Odom. Their criminal history, coupled with their involvement with the noise complaint on the night of Donald's murder, allowed the Mobile Police to paint the picture they needed.

Twenty-three-year-old Ralph Hayes had previously been arrested for burglary and marijuana possession, serving four months of a year-long term in 1976. Likewise, twenty-two-year-old Jimmy Edgar spent a year in prison for carnal knowledge and burglary in 1979. And while twenty-six-year-old Johnny had never been arrested, Mobile Police officers were already informing newspaper reporters that the men appeared to be "junkies"—casting the trio in a poor light from the start. Newspapers reported that the inside of the apartment reflected "boisterous living," noting the "mattress on the floor, rock culture posters on the wall and stereo records heaped against the wall"—nearly crimes in themselves, judging by the police depictions.

To make matters worse, a witness came forward describing having seen at least two men and two women drunk in a pulpwood truck around the camphor tree just days after Michael's murder.

The witness reported that as the men stumbled around the truck, one turned to the other and said, "What did you hang that nigger for?" to which the other replied, "Man, you know I didn't hang that nigger. Don't be saying nothing like that." The men—most likely Ralph Hayes and one of the Edgar brothers (the witness knew that they were Cajun and had been previously picked up for questioning)—had joked about Michael Donald's murder, though the laughter would soon subside for both Ralph Hayes and the Edgars.

The police apprehended their suspects in the middle of the night, taking Jimmy and Johnny from their grandmother's home and Ralph from his mother's.

While being transported to the police station, one of the three asked, "How many you'all going to charge for this murder?" to which the officer replied, "As many as did it."

After a pause, the man whispered, "There was about nine of us out there."

Most likely, the man—whether it was Jimmy, Johnny, or Ralph (the name was omitted)—was referring to the number of people present at the Dauphin Street apartment on the night of Ralph's domestic disturbance with his girlfriend, Linda.

Still, the reply was ominous, particularly from an innocent man.

On March 27, Ralph Hayes and the Edgar brothers were escorted into the courtroom amid representatives from the black community, as well as policemen and plainclothes officers. Mobile County District Judge Sullivan set the bail at $250,000 for each defendant, ignoring arguments from Ralph Hayes's lawyer—the only defense lawyer who bothered to show up—that the bail was excessive, and none of the three could even afford to pay $50,000, let alone five times that amount. Initially, the judge refused to budge, though a month later he agreed to lower the bail.

When the case went to the grand jury, twenty-seven-year-old Johnny Ray Kelly—the cab passenger in question—informed the jury that he had observed "the trio near the area where Donald's body was found at about the time when the black man was killed around 2:30 a.m." Kelly claimed that he had heard "two of the three bragg[ing] about having just attacked a black man who owed Hayes money for some pills."

Kelly continued his false testimony, assuring the jury that he had viewed Ralph Hayes "with a large blood spot on his shirt" and Jimmy "cleaning his fingernails with a bloody pocketknife." Later, he claimed Ralph had bragged that he had "hospital-whipped a nigger's ass."

Other witnesses quickly discredited the tale, and Kelly—who had a police record himself—was later accused of using his testimony as leverage for his own legal woes. However, his legal troubles only worsened once he was indicted for perjury.

Police Chief Wilbur Williams explained:

Well, the long and short of that story is Johnny's uncle was a police captain at a neighboring police department at Prichard, which borders the north side of Mobile. This captain had been hanging around the police department throughout the investigation. Johnny had three burglary charges pending against him in circuit court, and had he been convicted on any of those burglaries, he was facing the Habitual Offender Act, twenty to life. So he was looking for help. But he didn't find any. Instead, Johnny Ray Kelly was charged with two counts of perjury for falsely testifying against Ralph and Jimmy and Johnny. We produced enough evidence to convict him and he was given two life sentences in prison. I think he died there.

Hayes and the Edgar brothers were brought in front of the grand jury on June 5, 1981, though without the testimony of Johnny Ray Kelly, the jury declared a "No Bill," citing insubstantial evidence to prosecute. It was the same ruling the Tuscaloosa jury had found against the mob that murdered Dan Pippen Jr. and A. T. Harden nearly fifty years before.

Much to the Mobile Police Department's frustration, the men were released and the investigation returned to square one. However, at least one police officer was pleased with the outcome—Wilbur Williams. Williams played an integral role in proving Ralph Hayes and the Edgar brothers' innocence, believing from the start that they didn't have the right men in custody.

"My initial assessment was that this was some bad stuff, and that it was very likely the Klan was involved," Williams began. "Michael was hung, and it was the traditional hangman's noose, thirteen wraps. We were successful in getting the charges dropped against Ralph and Jimmy and Johnny, finally producing enough evidence once we discredited Johnny Ray Kelly. And eventually, we convinced District Attorney Chris Galanos that we were headed in the wrong direction, too."

"But how did this all get put together?" Williams continued, referring to the arrests of three innocent men. "Well, I want to believe there was some kind of conscious effort to frame Jimmy, Johnny and Ralph Hayes, just to have it wrapped up. But what was the ulterior motive? I'm not absolutely totally convinced there's not a semblance of a chance that somebody said, 'We need to give this to somebody else. This doesn't need to fall on the Klan,'" he admitted. "Now, I can't prove that, it's just one of those alternatives floating around. Personally, I care to choose that it was just an opportunity to wrap it up, lazy police work, incompetent police work—whatever you want to label it—that caused it to go out in this direction. I was never convinced it was some kind of cover-up."

"But all along," he concluded, "my first impression, my second impression, my third impression, and every impression in between was that the Ku Klux Klan was involved."

A memo from the Mobile FBI office to the director accurately expressed the disappointment that rippled throughout the black community upon the release of Ralph Hayes and the Edgar brothers:

"Black leaders in the Mobile area have been following the case closely since its inception and with the release of the 3 white males publically expressed shock over the turn of events."

Demonstrations were held outside the courthouse, pamphlets and flyers distributed encouraging "firebombing and shooting 'Klansmen-looking targets.'"

A copy of one of the racially motivated propaganda flyers depicted a white man raping a black woman while a speech cloud above his head reads: "I freed my 3 Klan men with FBI and police court help for hanging ya'lls nigger Donald, they cut Donald's penis off and stuck it in his mouth, too."

The claim that Michael Donald's genitals were in any way harmed is unfounded. According to the autopsy report, Michael's genitals appeared unharmed—one of the few areas of his body that could receive such an assessment.

The flyer also depicted an illustration of a black man hanging from a tree, alongside an arrow identifying the corpse as Michael's. Above the white man is a second speech cloud that reads: "I rape nigger women too." Beneath him, the black woman shouts, "Save me Black Brother!" and "Please don't rape me white man, black men please help protect me."

Below the drawing is a call to arms: "Young black men . . . stop hangings and rapes. Firebombs are made from gas filled bottles and rags. Make and light up firebombs and throw firebombs at night at any white klanman looking target you see. Like the old year out and the new year in, any black man with a gun should shoot at any white klanman looking target at night in June or July or August. The first shot is the signal for every black man to shoot and burn . . . Firebomb Uncle Tom preachers churches and black sellout politicians too. Struggle to win."

Anger continued to mount, and feeling that the Mobile Police were not fully communicating with them, the African-American community waited for someone to come to their defense.

In April 1981, Reverend Jesse Jackson arrived in Mobile.

"Don't let them break your spirit!" Jackson cried to a crowd eight thousand strong.

At the conclusion of his speech, Jackson and hundreds of other black men and women revived the unbroken spirit of the civil rights movement and marched along Herndon Avenue with Jackson brandishing an ax, determined to chop down the camphor tree from which Michael was hanged.

That day, the crowd did manage to bring a tree to the ground, though it was not the camphor tree.

According to reporter Michael Wilson, the newspapers had purposefully photographed the wrong tree "so that only the detectives and the killers would know which one held the body."

However, Wilbur Williams disputed the claim.

"We never had anyone intentionally photograph the wrong tree," he chuckled. Williams explained how an officer had misidentified the tree for a photograph that later appeared in a national magazine, leading Jesse Jackson's crowd to believe they were chopping down the right one.

"But they never did chop the right tree," Williams explained, "because the last time I was over there it was still standing."

In the months following Michael Donald's death, the city began its return to normal. There was no further violence, though Mobile's black community did not soon forget.

Nor did the police.

Two years later, on Thursday, June 16, 1983, the federal authorities pulled up to the Hudson Service Station on Battleship Parkway in Mobile, Alabama, and carried out their warrant.

Charged for conspiracy against the rights of citizens, twenty-eight-year-old Henry Francis Hays, residing at 115 Herndon Avenue—the man who had chatted with police on the night of the murder, as well as assisted the cab driver in collecting his fare—was placed in handcuffs by federal agents.

Two years prior, the police had come close in arresting his neighbor, Ralph Hayes.

But the police simply had the wrong Hayes on Herndon Avenue. It was an honest enough mistake. The mailman probably made it all the time.

SEVENTH LOOP
A BEATING IN BALDWIN COUNTY

Mobile, March 17, 1981

While they was arguing about whether they should kill me or not they decided to flip a coin.

On Tuesday, March 17, just four days before Michael Donald's death, Kenneth Jones, a white male identified as a homosexual, got off from work and picked up a cup of coffee at the McDonald's on the corner of Washington and Government Streets before stopping for a drink at Crew's Pub on St. Francis.

"I had a couple of beers there," Jones recounted. "I came out and I struck up a conversation with these two white guys who was parked next to me. They suggested that maybe we, why don't we go get a beer down at the Royal Club. So I got in the car with them."

It proved to be a near-fatal mistake.

Instead of turning right, the man in the driver's seat—wearing jeans and a nylon jacket—careened the black Buick Wildcat through the tunnel leading to Baldwin County, in the opposite direction of the Royal Club.

"What the devil's going on?" Jones asked as he sat in the backseat with a greasy-haired man in a red shirt. The man pulled a knife on him and said, "This is what['s] going on"

"He put the knife to my throat," Jones continued, "and made me get down on the floor board of the car and actually made me lay my head down on the seat while he held the knife to my throat."

The car veered north onto Highway 225 before turning east just past Highway 31 a few miles deeper into the wilderness. As they pulled onto a dirt road, one of the men grabbed a rifle from the trunk. The two men pulled Jones from the backseat, smashing his glasses and robbing him. Jones recalled the men discussing whether or not they should kill him. Finding themselves unable to come to a decision, one of the men laid down his rifle and began beating Jones and smacking his face.

"All the while," Jones reported, "he did not even allow me to protect myself because they kept telling me they would cut my throat then, if I didn't put my hands down by my sides."

The man wielding the knife cut off a portion of Jones's beard, proving the blade's sharpness.

Kenneth Jones's shirt was ripped from his back, and "while they was arguing about whether they should kill me or not they decided to flip a coin. [A]t first, [one of the men] pulled a coin out of his own pocket and then he decided that since they was going to rob me anyway, I should supply the coin."

Jones handed over the quarter that would decide his fate while the man with the rifle told the victim to continue stripping down, demanding he remove his shoes, socks, and pants. After taking thirty dollars from Jones's wallet, the two men continued their conversation as to whether or not they should kill him, at which point the larger of the men decided killing him was unnecessary. The thinner man disagreed, explaining how he'd "done this one time before and they'd let the guy go and three days later, his house was burned."

As they continued arguing, Jones was ordered to get on his knees and pray.

"I did a pretty good job of praying," he admitted, "and [name omitted] turned to put my clothes in the car and [name omitted] turned around to lay the rifle back down and I took this opportunity since both heads were turned away, to make a dash into the brush in the woods."

Jones ran as the car peeled off, only returning to the scene once he was certain his attackers had fled. He grabbed what clothes remained before sprinting to a nearby store, where the manager called the sheriff. It was dark, and by the time the sheriff and the victim returned to the scene, they found only tire tracks and scattered footprints. A Mobile Police car arrived soon after and drove the victim back to Mobile, where Jones was checked into a hospital. He was discharged the following Sunday, by which point a second victim—Michael Donald—had already been driven to the same spot and murdered.

It was almost as if Jones's attackers had been practicing.

Years later, in June 1983, a Buick Wildcat was recovered, half-buried in a weeded lot. The back right tire was flat, and the knee-high weeds had overtaken the majority of the back end of the car. The car's hood was removed, as was the engine and various other parts. Upon locating it, investigators transported the car to Duke's Garage and Bodyshop on 600 St. Anthony Street for further examination.

FBI agents observed any number of things crowding the backseat of the Wildcat: drink containers, an empty transmission fluid container, paper towels, two auto belts, a cardboard box, a paper bag, a chain, and nuts and bolts, among other objects. The front seat held much of the same, including a rag and a beer can. Neither did the trunk hold much of interest: a toy mailbox, two beer cans, wood glue, swimming trunks, shotgun shell casings, one brick, and a homemade wrench.

But most noteworthy was not what was obviously apparent, but what was to be seen under the FBI's microscopes: a single Negroid hair sample taken from a bag of debris in the trunk.

Other items related to the case were taken into the FBI lab as well, including Michael's T-shirt, blue jeans, jacket, shirt, sweater, undershorts, socks, shoes, a noose, as well as a length of rope—all of which pathologist Dr. Riddick had removed prior to the autopsy.

The FBI took great care in describing Michael's clothing.

His T-shirt was white and stained, size 38–40, brand "Golden Comfort." His blue jeans were 100 percent cotton Levi Strauss, size 30 X 33. His belt was leather, though his Led Zeppelin belt buckle was covered in dirt. His blue-lined nylon jacket was made of 100 percent nylon as well as 100 percent cotton in the lining. A size medium. Its tag read "Royal Knight." The jacket's left sleeve was torn, and there was another tear on the right shoulder. Michael's short-sleeved brown plaid shirt retained six buttons, though the second from the top was missing. Brand "Mad Man." His gray V-neck pullover was also of the "Royal Knight" brand, and it, too, was stained with blood and dust. Jockey briefs and size nine Converse shoes were all that remained of Michael Donald.

But most puzzling of all was the belt buckle. Was Michael Donald a Led Zeppelin fan? And if so, what do we make of a young African-American sporting a belt buckle for an all-white band? Was it a clue to Michael Donald's own colorblindness—that he judged not on the color of one's skin but on the content of one's music—or was it simply a coincidence?

We know little of Michael Donald's interactions with whites prior to his murder. An FBI interview revealed that according to one of Michael's acquaintances, "Donald did not have the inclination to involve himself with any particular white friends." The source went on to conclude that he "knew no individuals who were white who were friends of Michael Donald." While this certainly does not imply that Michael Donald had any preconceived negative feelings toward whites, it does point to the possibility of a lack of interaction between races. Michael's interactions with whites may have been limited, though this did not keep him from trusting people regardless of color—a progressive view that would cost him his life.

The FBI report included a hand-drawn sketch of the noose, the top section apparently cut by Dr. Riddick, though the sketch artist labeled the cut "tied together" to explain that it had been uncut at the time of its use. The sketch also noted the "yellowish color" and the "melted end of rope" dangling down toward the lower half of the page. The only inaccuracy is in the number of loops: eleven in the sketch, two short of the thirteen used to take the breath from Michael Donald.

Throughout the spring and summer of 1983, the Mobile Police, in conjunction with the FBI, continued to conjure life from the lifeless.

Their top priority: examining the forensic evidence left behind.

Police sent an eleven-page inventory of items relevant to the case to the Alabama Department of Forensic Sciences in the hopes that a microscopic view might reveal previously overlooked evidence.

They sent boots and shirts and jackets, bags containing sticks, a key, and rope. A baseball bat, a tissue. Urine, blood, hair. Fingernails, swabs. A suede jacket. Soil from Causeway. Rope. Cups. Cigarette butts.

Meanwhile, the FBI turned over Michael's various belongings to the district attorney.

One gray sweater, one blue jacket. Tennis shoes. Socks. Underwear. Rope from the tree. Rope from the noose. A black wallet. Soil samples from Baldwin County.

While the lab work played an integral role in the investigation, equally important was the television footage captured by WKRG-TV on the morning of the murder.

The FBI contacted the news station and, upon reviewing the taped footage, noticed Bennie Jack Hays—Henry Hays's father and a known Klansmen—as well as various other Klansmen lurking in the background just behind the crowd.

While the news footage offered no definitive answers, it raised more questions worth considering.

And for the FBI, the news clip of Grand Titan Bennie Jack Hays at the murder scene on the morning following Donald's death was reason enough to give the Klan a second look.

Even more damning was the picture taken on Herndon Avenue just hours after the murder. In it, Bennie Jack Hays, James "Tiger" Knowles, Henry Hays, and Henry's mother, Opal, are all seen huddled around the side of what appears to be Knowles's pickup truck.

And just behind them, a dark-colored car, perhaps a Buick Wildcat.

EIGHTH LOOP
A KLAVERN IN THE WOODS

Mobile, March 18–21, 1981

Beat me just don't kill me . . .

On March 18, 1981—as Michael Donald clocked in at the *Mobile Register* for the last time—United Klans of America (UKA) Klavern Unit 900 met at Grand Titan Bennie Jack Hays's residence on Gunn Road in Theodore, Alabama, just a few miles outside of Mobile. Present were Henry Hays, James "Tiger" Knowles, as well as various other Klansmen including William O'Connor, Frank Cox, Teddy Kyzar, Thaddeus Betancourt, and Frank Ginocchio. The group met on a weekly basis, and while there was rarely new business to discuss, on that particular night, there was.

The ongoing trial of the shooting death of Birmingham Police Sergeant Gene Ballard had caused quite a stir throughout Birmingham two years prior, so much so that the trial required a change of venue to Mobile, where the defense felt suspect Josephus Anderson stood a better chance for acquittal. In the midst of the trial, Klansman Thaddeus Betancourt cut out a newspaper clipping reporting the trial and placed it in the Klavern scrapbook for all to read.

"I was under the impression at the time that it was the type of material that the Klan was interested in," he later confessed.

The Klan watched from afar, anticipating a hotly contested trial.

On Wednesday, March 18, two days prior to Michael's death and a day after Kenneth Jones was beaten in Baldwin County, the Klavern met on Gunn Road, as always, and in response to Anderson's trial, discussed what should be done if the killer got off.

As noted in Morris Dees and Steve Fiffer's *A Season for Justice*, Henry Hays quoted William O'Connor as stating, "There ought to be a damned nigger hung if this guy is turned loose."

The others agreed, and after the meeting broke, Bennie Jack Hays, his son Henry, and seventeen-year-old James "Tiger" Knowles began speculating "what people would think if they found a nigger hanging from a tree in Mobile County."

While the details of the conversation remain unknown, Tiger Knowles later testified that Bennie Jack specifically told them "not to do anything until after Friday" on account of a real estate deal in which he planned to sell his Herndon Avenue apartments. Tiger claimed to interpret Bennie Jack's pronouncement as a direct order, which implied that *after* the real estate deal was complete that Friday, they were free to act.

On Friday, March 20, as several Klansmen and a few neighbors studied their cards inside Henry Hays's Herndon Avenue apartment, the ten o'clock news reported just what the Klansmen feared—the trial of Josephus Anderson had ended in a deadlock. The jury consisting of five men and seven women—eleven blacks and one white—had been incapable of finding Anderson guilty.

The Klavern had planned to burn a cross on the courthouse lawn in the event that Anderson's trial ended in what the Klan considered a displeasing verdict—a deadlock or acquittal.

But upon hearing the news, a few of the Klansmen situated around the card table on Herndon Avenue had already begun feeling as if burning a cross was far too weak a response. In a witness report dated July 12, 1983, an unidentified woman who had been sitting around the table that night recalled Hays and Knowles being "mad about a trial" because a "nigger" had not received the conviction they had hoped for.

But it was Denise Hays's testimony that proved most damning.

Henry Hays's ex-wife later informed the jury that once Henry heard the news he grumbled, "Goddamn nigger got off," at which point Henry and Tiger Knowles excused themselves from the room, slipping into Hays's 1973 black Buick Wildcat and disappearing into the night.

The Klan had prepared for this outcome.

Not only had Henry, Tiger, and Bennie Jack discussed possible retaliation for an unfavorable outcome, but earlier in the day, Henry, Tiger, and fellow Klansman Frank Cox—Henry's brother-in-law—had taken action, driving to Frank's parents' home to retrieve a twenty-four-foot nylon rope suitable for hanging.

After retrieving the rope, they made one final stop at fellow Klansman Johnny Matthew Jones's trailer in nearby Theodore. Jones owned a .22 pistol—a good choice for easy concealment—and Henry Hays and Tiger Knowles said they needed to borrow it for the night.

As Henry, Frank, and Tiger began their drive back to Herndon Avenue after assembling the necessary materials, Tiger Knowles sat in the passenger seat and began working the rope through his fingers, using Frank Cox's lighter to burn the end to keep it from unraveling.

During the trial, when asked what he had done in the front seat and why, Tiger replied simply, "I was tying a hangman's noose for the purpose of hanging someone."

Despite other timelines that argue that Henry Hays and Tiger Knowles left the Herndon Avenue apartment later in the evening, Knowles testified that he and Hays slipped into the Buick Wildcat at around 10:00 p.m., prior to the end of the basketball game, looking for "a black person to kill."

Hays drove the Wildcat along the city streets, eyeing potential victims, nearly stopping for an elderly black man talking on a pay phone, though he and Knowles eventually decided that he might prove to be too much of a hassle owing to his distance from the car.

"And he was real close to a telephone," Knowles recalled. "And he was talking on the phone. And so we didn't—we decided not to grab him, because he was on the phone. It might cause too much of a commotion."

Knowles would later describe their coasting down Davis Avenue and side streets for between twenty to thirty minutes before coming across their victim—a shadowed figure walking in the direction of the Gulf station.

Most likely, Knowles's timeline is slightly off because at 10:30 p.m. Michael was still in Betty Wyatt's home, watching the end of the game.

What is known for certain is that sometime between 10:30 and 11:15 p.m., Henry Hays pulled to the side of the road and Tiger Knowles leaned out to call to the young black man walking past them.

"I asked him if he knew where a nightclub was and he started to direct me. I asked him to come closer and he leaned over and I pulled the gun out," Knowles later testified. "I told him to be quiet and he would not be hurt."

Years prior to Knowles's testimony, Michael's sister Cecelia Perry informed the *Mobile Register*, "You could tell him to do something and he never talked back or argued. He'd grumble a little, but he never disobeyed."

True to form, Michael stayed quiet just as he'd been told.

It didn't matter.

Rick Kerger, Henry Hays's attorney, found various holes in Tiger Knowles's testimony.

"I don't think there's much question that Henry committed the murder," Kerger admitted decades after the trial. "But I think things just got off track. I don't think Henry intended to commit the murder. I don't think Tiger did, either. They had a gun and a short box cutter, and they had about twenty-feet of rope. And these pine trees, the lowest limbs are fifteen to eighteen feet in the air. You're going to need thirty-feet of rope to hang anyone under those conditions, to make the noose and all."

Kerger offered further proof to his theory that it was simply a stupid act that turned wildly out of control. He noted how Hays and Knowles didn't even have any means to bind Michael Donald's hands, nor were they willing to shoot him.

"During the cross-examination I asked Knowles, 'Well how were you going to kill him?' and he said he didn't know. Well, if you're going to go kill somebody, one would think you're going to have thought that out," Kerger pointed out.

Kerger went on to describe how Michael had burst free once the car was parked in Baldwin County, how Michael had muscled the gun away from Knowles.

"And then a fight took place," Kerger continued. "Henry had had his hand injured in a work-related injury a couple of weeks before, so he was essentially fighting with one hand. Tiger was a beefy, not particular physically fit seventeen-year-old, and Donald was fearful for his life. So, [Henry and Tiger] were getting the worst of it for a while. Then somebody got a piece of wood and clubbed Donald until he stopped, and then they took the rope and choked him to death, then took the body back and frankly, they didn't know what to do with the body so they put it on Herndon Avenue because they figured nobody would expect to find it there," Kerger concluded.

"And sure enough, it worked better than they thought."

❖

These are the moments reserved only for speculation.

With Michael dead, we are left only with the testimony of his killers, only half the story.

We will, for instance, never fully understand if Michael hesitated, if he considered running, whether or not he actually believed those men would shoot him as he walked down the Mobile streets. We will never comprehend those initial moments, how he accounted for the violent act or why he felt it was wrought upon him. Nor will we ever know if the radio was on or off during the car ride, what song might have been playing, if the radio reported the jury's deadlocked decision or the basketball score. We know nothing of the temperature within that car, if the windows were open or closed, what food wrappers lay scattered on the floorboards where, just days prior, another man had been held captive with a knife to his neck.

What we do know is what Tiger Knowles tells us.

How he and Michael sat side by side on the red vinyl backseat of the Buick Wildcat while Hays drove them to Baldwin County, following the route he'd driven just days prior when they'd abducted Kenneth Jones. And how at some point during the drive, Knowles ordered Michael to empty his pockets.

"He gave me a wallet," Knowles claimed, "and I laid it on the floorboard of the car."

Throughout the drive, a terrified Michael repeated, "I can't believe this is happening. I'll do anything you want. Beat me just don't kill me."

"He kept saying, 'Please don't kill me,'" Knowles remembered thoughtfully.

He would later testify that Hays had told Michael, "You know all those little nigger kids that's been getting killed up in Atlanta? Well, a lot of people think the Klan is behind it. But we are not. You know the same thing could happen to you."

Chances are Michael was aware of the Atlanta killings. The murders had been reported for weeks, even gracing the front page of the *Mo-*

bile Register on Michael's last day on earth. The article reported that the supposed Atlanta killer had called Reverend Earl Paulk describing "a voice that would not leave him alone"—further evidence of a psychopath with no ties to the Klan.

Soon after, the Atlanta killings were charged to African-American Wayne Williams, though there is still much controversy over whether he actually committed all the murders for which he was implicated.

Meanwhile, inside the Buick Wildcat, the pleading continued.

"Please don't kill me. You can do anything you want . . ."

After arriving at a deserted patch of land in Baldwin County, Henry Hays put the Wildcat in park and ordered Michael out of the car.

"Donald acted like he was a crazed mad man," Knowles recounted. "I had the gun in my hand and he jumped me."

"And we just—after fighting him for just a few moments, we got him down," Knowles said. "And he was just—he was just lying there like a crazed animal after us fighting him for a while. And Henry went and got the rope. And between the both of us, we got it around his neck and we pulled the rope tight. Henry put his foot on Michael's head to secure it to the ground so we could pull the rope tight. And he just— he just lied there. And I grabbed at the end of the rope. And Henry got a limb and he was hitting Donald with it. And I pulled the rope . . . He kept getting up and falling back down . . . Henry kept hitting him . . . And I had the end of the rope, the opposite end of the rope. And finally Donald just fell."

Tiger recounted how Henry continued tugging at the rope, keeping a boot pressed firmly against Michael's lifeless body.

"[I]t was like he was enjoying this," Tiger added.

Knowles admitted that he and Hays hit Michael with a limb over a hundred times. The autopsy report concurred with Knowles's testimony, revealing that the greatest damage was inflicted to Michael's head and upper torso.

"Ohio" Woodcut, originally printed in Ryland Randolph's *The Independent Monitor*, 1868.

Tom Shipp and Abe Smith, Marion, Indiana, August 7, 1930. Courtesy of the Richard A. Greene Photograph Collection, Archives & Special Collections, Ball State University Libraries.

Above: Grand Wizard Robert Shelton and United Klans of America members, April 23, 1965. Courtesy of the W. S. Hoole Special Collections Library, The University of Alabama.

Left: Sergeant Gene Ballard in police uniform, 1970s. Courtesy of Kathy Sutton.

Leave Middle School for Senior High

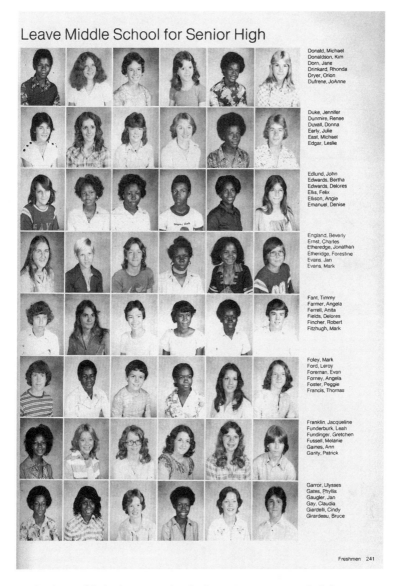

Donald, Michael
Donaldson, Kim
Dorn, Jane
Drinkard, Rhonda
Dryer, Orion
Dufrene, JoAnne

Duke, Jennifer
Dunmire, Renee
Duvall, Donna
Early, Julie
East, Michael
Edgar, Leslie

Edlund, John
Edwards, Bertha
Edwards, Delores
Ellis, Felix
Ellison, Angie
Emanuel, Denise

England, Beverly
Ernst, Charles
Etheredge, Jonathan
Etheridge, Forestine
Evans, Jan
Evans, Mark

Fant, Timmy
Farmer, Angela
Ferrell, Anita
Fields, Delores
Fincher, Robert
Fitzhugh, Mark

Foley, Mark
Ford, Leroy
Foreman, Evan
Forney, Angela
Foster, Peggie
Francis, Thomas

Franklin, Jacqueline
Funderburk, Leah
Fundinger, Gretchen
Fussell, Melanie
Gaines, Ann
Garity, Patrick

Garror, Ulysses
Gates, Phyllis
Gaugler, Jan
Gay, Claudia
Giardelli, Cindy
Girardeau, Bruce

Freshmen 241

Michael Donald's freshman yearbook photo, 1977. Top row, far left.
Courtesy of Carmen Kearley and the Murphy High School Library.

Above: United Klans of America Rally, Mobile, Alabama, 1977. Photo by Dave Hamby, courtesy of and copyrighted by the *Mobile Press-Register.*

Left: Rare photo of Michael Donald. Courtesy of Wilbur Williams.

The lynching of Michael Donald, March 20, 1981. Courtesy of Wilbur Williams.

Michael Donald murder scene, Baldwin County, 1981. Courtesy of and copyrighted by the *Mobile Press-Register.*

The thirteen-looped noose. *Azalea City News* Collection, University of South Alabama Archives.

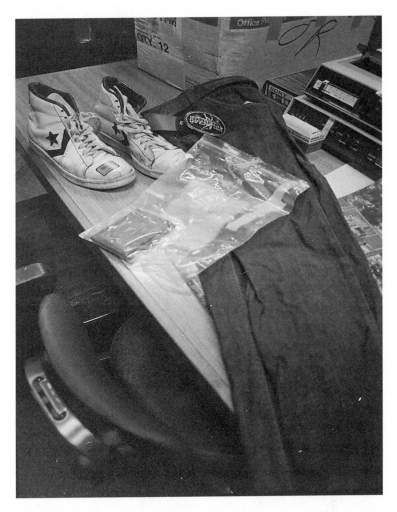

Michael Donald's Converse tennis shoes, Led Zeppelin belt buckle, jeans, and wallet. *Azalea City News* Collection, University of South Alabama Archives.

Left: Henry Hays led into court, June 16, 1983. Courtesy of and copyrighted by the *Mobile Press-Register.*

Below: Henry F. Hays, February 1984. Courtesy of and copyrighted by the *Mobile Press-Register.*

Grand Titan Bennie Jack Hays and Opal Hays, father and mother of Henry
Hays, February 1984. Courtesy of and copyrighted by the *Mobile Press-
Register.*

James "Tiger" Knowles, February 1988. Courtesy of and copyrighted by the *Mobile Press-Register*.

Michael Donald's brother, Stanley Donald, at street dedication, May 16, 2006. Courtesy of and copyrighted by the *Mobile Press-Register*.

The *Mobile Register* vividly reported the brutality with which Hays and Knowles "took turns hitting him with the limb and tightening the rope" until Michael eventually collapsed.

"Donald fell face flat on the ground and then we both got the rope and dragged him to the rear of the car," continued Knowles. "We put the body in the trunk. He was laying on his back and Hays had the utility knife."

As they stood in the clearing, peering down at the battered body, Tiger Knowles whispered, "Think he's dead?"

To which Henry Hays responded, "I don't know but I'm gonna make sure."

Hunching over, Hays slit Michael's throat three times with the utility knife.

Once the bloodied body was in the trunk of the Wildcat, they slowly headed back toward Herndon Avenue, stopping first at Johnny Matthew Jones's trailer to return the borrowed gun.

Tiger Knowles never spoke of the conversation he and Hays shared as they returned to Herndon Avenue with Michael's body in the trunk. Knowles was only seventeen at the time of the murder, Henry ten years his elder.

Nearly fifty years prior in Tuscaloosa, a masked mob decided to send a message that blacks couldn't murder whites without recourse.

And in 1981, Henry Hays and Tiger Knowles were sending the same message, though they also wanted to make it clear that blacks had no business serving on juries, either.

Henry and Tiger had already sent their message to one black man, but one wasn't enough.

They wanted to make sure everyone heard it.

This is not the story Henry Hays told police on April 20, 1981, a month after the murder.

In Hays's version, he had spent the majority of the evening of March 20 playing Spades and watching television with friends. Sometime around 1:00 a.m.—after overhearing Ralph Hayes's domestic dispute with Linda Odom—he allegedly called the police to report a noise complaint, then wandered over to the cab driver who that had been stiffed his fare. After he and the driver knocked on a few doors and were unable to retrieve the fare, Henry returned to his apartment and watched Farrah Fawcett in *Saturn 3,* as well as the opening minutes of Clint Eastwood's *The Enforcer.*

He admitted leaving his apartment one last time before going to bed, driving to a nearby gas station with his friends to pick up a pack of cigarettes.

Henry Hays's unexpected concern for the stiffed cab driver served as a much-needed alibi.

In the 1983 appeals process, Hays noted: "[The cab driver and I] walked around the driveway between 115 and 111 and went around and there wasn't anybody in the other apartment because we went right to Linda Odom's apartment because they had several people coming and going all the time," Henry explained. "So I just naturally assumed that if anybody, you know, was going to that apartment, you know, that apartment building, they would be going to their apartment. So I went up with the white cab driver and knocked on the door. And Linda Odom came to the door."

Hays went on to describe the conversation that followed, how Linda Odom claimed there was only one male in the house, so Henry asked for him to come to the door so the cab driver could get a look at him. Moments later, a greasy-haired man came into view.

"So this is the first time I'd ever seen Ralph Hayes," Henry Hays admitted.

It was the first time the true murderer gazed upon the man who nearly took the fall.

But Henry Hays had arranged other alibis as well.

Linda Johnson, a neighbor and friend of the Hays's family, confirmed Henry Hays's interactions with the cab driver. She also confirmed his going out just after midnight.

"He drove to Delchamps and got some Cokes and come back to the house," she testified. "He came back with some Cokes and . . . another bag of chips."

Yet Henry Hays had also gone to great lengths to concoct his own alibi for the precise moments in which Michael was murdered, stating: "I went to the ComPac Store; well, 7-Eleven Store . . . I went up to the one on Catherine Street down on Catherine and Old Shell. It's on the corner there right by McGill School . . . Me, Tiger and Teddy [Kyzar] went to the store . . . See, I was on workman's comp, I had some food stamps and stuff like that, you know, and we got some Cokes, some Mountain Dew and cigarettes, and we played some pinball. They had one of those *Star Track* [sic] pinball machines, I remember that. And we played a couple of games of pinball and then went back to the house. We was gone thirty, forty minutes or so."

The similarities between the actual events of Michael Donald's night and the partially fabricated events of Henry Hays's are uncanny.

Both observed a game of cards, both left for a pack of cigarettes.

The only difference: One was black, one was white, and one returned home in the morning.

NINTH LOOP
A CROSS, A DUMMY, A PHONE CALL

Mobile, March 21, 1981

What appeared to be a dummy hanging in a tree . . .

At a little after midnight, Klansmen Frank Cox and Teddy Kyzar drove
to the Mobile County Courthouse and lit a burning cross on the courthouse lawn as a so-called diversionary tactic. Yet burning a cross on
the courthouse lawn just hours after a racially charged deadlocked trial
and brutal murder seems, in retrospection, far less tactical than the
Klan may have initially thought.

Nevertheless, district attorney investigator Bob Eddy claimed this
"tactic" was actually quite common for the Klan.

"It was just typical for them to do things like that," he explained.
"Case after case, they did the same thing. Do one thing one place and
something a lot worse somewhere else."

While it's difficult to discern the exact order of events, reports show
that at 2:45 a.m., two private security officers were driving their routine patrol near the intersection of Royal and Church Streets when
they noticed flames coming from the courthouse lawn. The security
guards stopped the car to examine the fire more closely, stumbling
across what appeared to be a three-foot-tall, two-foot-wide cross that

was constructed entirely of burlap and wires. The poorly built fire was already smoldering by the time the security guards arrived.

At 2:52 a.m., the report was radioed to a Mobile Police officer, who was called to investigate the supposed cross burning. Upon arriving at the scene, he noticed that the fire had already been extinguished and that if he hadn't been told a cross had been burning, he would not have known that the fire had taken that shape. All he observed was a small "smoldering pile of what appeared to be burlap material."

Teddy Kyzar recalled preparing for the cross burning soon after Hays and Knowles returned to the Herndon Avenue apartment at a little past midnight.

"And we went down to the back of 111 Herndon, the old burned house, went back towards the back of the garage," Kyzar explained. "Frank reached into the back of the garage and got the cross that was already made . . . Tiger reached in where the cross was and got a gallon of diesel fuel and put it in the back of the pickup truck. Frank went around to the driver's side and I automatically got in on the passenger side, and we pulled out and started out of the driveway."

Klansmen Frank Cox and Teddy Kyzar circled the Mobile County Courthouse three times before Cox decided it was time to act.

"That's where I want it," Cox informed Teddy, pointing to a spot on the lawn.

"I still never did ask why the cross was going to be burned or where," Teddy explained. "And when he told me that's where he wanted it, I got out of the truck, got the gallon of diesel fuel and cross out of the back of the pickup truck, ran up to the—close to the building, laid the cross down, soaked it down and used all the diesel fuel, stuck it up in the ground and made sure it was going to stand up straight."

The pudgy, glasses-wearing Teddy Kyzar lit the match and, grabbing the empty diesel jug, bumbled down Water Street, eventually spotting Frank Cox at a red light and leaping into the truck while the cross began crackling behind him.

Later, Teddy described how he and Cox had turned off at the Fair-hope exit, where they stopped at a Waffle House to use the pay phone. They were told to inform Henry Hays that the cross had been lit without incident, but upon reaching the phone, both men realized they didn't have the proper change.

While Frank Cox and Teddy Kyzar squealed off into the night, Hays and Knowles had a job of their own. Within two to four hours following the murder, the pair busily hoisted Michael Donald's body into the camphor tree just across the street from Hays's apartment on Herndon Avenue, quite near the site of Ralph Hayes's violent interactions with his girlfriend.

It's difficult to envision the scope of the scene in its entirety: a cross burning on the courthouse lawn, Ralph Hayes chasing his girlfriend into the night, a snoring cab driver, three police officers on Herndon Avenue, and Hays and Knowles pulling a yellow nylon rope through the Y of a camphor tree, raising a dead, bloodied body just a few inches above the ground.

The FBI files on the Michael Donald case—over one thousand pages available to the public—records countless statements of virtually every man, woman, and child in the vicinity of Herndon Avenue on the night of the murder. And yet despite the cab drivers, the fighting couples, the card games, the drunks, the drug users, the tenants, and the police officers, apparently no one witnessed anything to link Hays and Knowles to the crime.

The one witness who came closest was Linda Odom's friend who recalled seeing, "this black car in the back of the apartments and these two white guys came from somewhere."

The two white guys, most likely, were the murderers.

Yet despite the fact that Henry Hays was an admitted Klansman living just feet away from the tree on which Michael was hanged, and despite the fact that the property was owned by Henry Hays's father,

Grand Titan Bennie Jack Hays, it still took officers over two years to make an arrest.

One report noted that at 2:00 a.m., fresh from murdering Michael Donald, Henry Hays was the one to call the police on Ralph Hayes and Linda Odom, citing a domestic disturbance and a noise complaint. Brasher still, Hays apparently went outside to meet the officer and then proceeded to help the cab driver collect his fare in the hours between the murder and the hanging.

And all the while, just feet away, Michael Donald's body turned cold in the trunk of a Buick Wildcat, all thirteen loops wrapped tight.

In a witness statement dated May 11, 1981, a white female reported what she observed after waking early the morning following the murder.

After a night of partying, the woman woke between 4:30 and 5:00 a.m., at which point she rose and began riding her bicycle to the nearby Time Saver Store for a drink. Her dog accompanied her, trotting alongside as she rode in the dark. She rode past Georgia Street to Old Shell Road, then on to Herndon and Springhill until eventually reaching the Time Saver Store. She purchased her drink and started home. But as she headed back down Herndon, she saw something she had not seen during her initial ride past, what "appeared to be a dummy hanging in a tree."

She remembered telling her dog that it was too early for Halloween.

It never crossed her mind that the body might be real, and so she continued riding back to her residence. Just across the street, she also spotted a "blue or red car parked with its trunk open."

Months later, this information, too, would prove invaluable.

On Saturday, March 21, 1981, the sun rose at 5:56 a.m.

District Attorney Chris Galanos winced, waking to a ringing phone.

"Hello?" Galanos asked groggily.

"Get down here now," barked Mobile Police Captain Vince Richardson, "we got a black man hanging from a tree."

Galanos arrived on Herndon Avenue approximately twenty to thirty minutes after the initial call.

"The body was being cut down by Dr. Riddick when I arrived," Galanos recalled. "I don't believe too many folks actually saw that body. It had already gone into rigor mortis. The sight was grotesque; the arms were sort of bent at the elbows. The victim's features were distorted, and I could not fathom the senselessness of the moment. From an investigative perspective, the noose was a huge piece of evidence. It was tied in what Captain Sam McClarty, Chief of Detectives, described as the classic Klan noose."

Galanos described the crowds that began gathering just after sunrise, large groups of "well-behaved but distraught African-American people."

"They were understandably hysterical," he remembered. "I shall never forget their anguish. They were weeping, wailing, people falling to the ground."

He paused.

"I remember staring at that body and being overwhelmed with a rush of emotions—the senselessness of the act, the impact on the community, and the enormity of the investigative task ahead. I sought and received the assistance of the FBI, and the ABI [Alabama Bureau of Investigation] so that by late Saturday afternoon or early Saturday evening, we had a task force. The lead agency, obviously, was the Mobile Police Department, but anything we needed from the federal government or state government, we got. I then realized the need to see all legitimate investigative assets and wondered how to coordinate our resources."

One of the district attorney's primary assets was investigator Bob Eddy. As the months passed, and as the anger continued to swell from within the black community, Galanos called upon his trusted friend to take a look at some of the information gathered by the black churches. Eddy, an investigator for the D.A.'s office who had experience working Klan cases, examined the materials, as well as the police reports, and began piecing together a theory.

"Basically, I just reexamined the obvious," he explained.

When discussing the possibility of a Klan connection, a lieutenant with the Mobile criminal investigation department informed Eddy that the Klan wasn't involved, despite the fact that known Klansmen lived on the same block as the hanging.

"The body was hung right across the street from their apartment," the lieutenant shrugged offhandedly. "They'd never do that. Too obvious."

But Eddy, like Police Chief Wilbur Williams, knew better than to give the Klan any benefit of the doubt.

However, it wasn't simply the proximity of the Klansmen to the body that spurred Eddy's interest. He knew something that the Tuscaloosa sheriff's department of 1933 hadn't—that proximity wasn't enough. A far more incriminating piece of evidence was the cross burning on the courthouse lawn on the same evening of the murder.

"In my experience working Klan cases, they always do something somewhere else when they did something they really don't want you to know about," Eddy explained. "For instance, in Birmingham, they'd break windows downtown and then bomb a place somewhere else. It was just typical for them to do things like that."

When Eddy asked the lieutenant whether he saw a connection between the murder and the cross burning, the lieutenant replied that he didn't think one was linked to the other.

Teddy Kyzar, one of the two men responsible for burning the cross, later testified to the contrary.

"[I]t was supposed to been set up for an alibi," Teddy explained.

Galanos recalled that after Ralph Hayes and the Edgar brothers were released, the focus shifted to the Klansmen, not only because of their proximity to the crime, but also because of news footage that clearly showed Bennie Jack walking up and down Herndon Avenue the morning Michael Donald was found.

"And according to testimony," Galanos continued, "Bennie Jack foolishly stared and stared at the body being cut down from the tree and said—and I'm only paraphrasing here—'Ain't that a pretty sight.'"

While the Mobile P.D. was less certain of his role, Eddy claimed to be one of the driving forces that continued putting full pressure on Henry Hays and the Klan.

After sifting through witness statements, Eddy stumbled across an inconsistency in the case. One statement described that on the night of the murder, two girls had spotted a black a car with its trunk open and two men talking to each other.

"But in the Hays boy's statement," Eddy began, "the car was parked in the driveway of the apartment complex. He told police that his car was parked in the driveway all night and he hadn't moved it until the next day around 10:00 a.m. But that didn't fit with what the girls were saying."

Eddy continued: "Plus, a photographer from the police department had taken pictures all up and down that street, and the strange thing was, the Hays boy's car was in those pictures at 6:00 a.m.—right there in the street with all the other cars. It wasn't in the driveway like he'd said. So I asked another investigator about that too, but he said not to worry too much about it, that the kid had probably 'just forgot.'"

But Eddy wasn't so easily convinced.

He wrote a memo to District Attorney Chris Galanos explaining his findings, noting, "If I were you, I'd form a grand jury and put every Klansmen in that apartment complex in front of it."

"I told Chris, 'If you get a grand jury, put them under oath, maybe we could break someone.'"

"So that's what we did," Galanos explained. "Once we had narrowed it down to a cast of characters, we just started dragging them in to the federal grand jury month after month after month because at some point we suspected, and fortunately, we were right, that one of them would break. And one did. And that was Tiger Knowles."

When asked about the seemingly obvious nature of the case, how the classic Klan noose and proximity of Klansmen to the murder seemed to point to KKK involvement, Eddy countered:

"[The Mobile Police Department] just hadn't worked a lot of Klan cases. They didn't know a lot of details about how the Klan worked . . . For instance, you could ask an investigator down there how one Klansman recognizes another and they wouldn't know. What they do is, they walk with their little finger and thumb in their pocket and other three fingers out. Just a little signal they had."

"But these cases are tough," he continued. "Lots of time you get tunnel vision. It's happened before. But it was obvious to me that we were overlooking too much, weren't taking statements seriously, weren't concentrating on what we really had and saw and heard. But if we're not going to concentrate on what we've got, then what are we going to concentrate on?"

"You know, it's one thing to *believe* that it was a Klan-related murder," Galanos later explained, "but it's another thing to prove it."

PART III Untangling

TENTH LOOP
A CONFESSION

Mobile, June 1983–February 1987

We're going home with this like men and women.

On Thursday, June 16, 1983, twenty-eight-year-old Henry Hays peered out the window of the Hudson Service Station, where he worked, and watched federal authorities step from their cars bearing handcuffs.

Miles away, nineteen-year-old James "Tiger" Knowles was faced with a similar scene.

While Henry remained mostly quiet following his arrest, Tiger— who claimed he had watched his family endure enough questioning— readily pleaded guilty to the charges of conspiracy and deprivation of a U.S. citizen's civil rights, implicating Henry Hays in his confession.

However, there are wildly different versions as to who actually broke the case.

According to FBI Special Agent Jim Bodman, the arrests of Tiger Knowles and Henry Hays came as a result of a phone call he received late one night from Knowles's attorney Holmes Whiddon.

The *Mobile Register* reports that after receiving a tip, Bodman told his wife he was going out for a while before driving to a downtown hotel where he, Whiddon, and Knowles met in the hotel parking lot in secret.

"You're leaning on the wrong one," Knowles informed Bodman, referring to the pressure placed on him and his family.

"You didn't mean for it to go as far as it did, did you?" Bodman asked, to which Knowles miserably confessed, "No, sir, we didn't mean to kill him."

Yet Police Chief Wilbur Williams is far from convinced that Bodman and the FBI brought the case to a close on their own.

In Williams's version, prior to the parking lot rendezvous, Whiddon and Knowles walked into the Mobile Police Station, where Whiddon discussed Knowles's confession with Mobile Police Captains Tommy Calhoun and John Phillips.

There, it was decided that Knowles's confession was, perhaps "too big for them," speculates Williams, and Knowles was told to confess to the FBI instead.

"That's how the case ended up at the FBI," Williams explained. Williams also noted that he has possession of Captain Tommy Calhoun's report, proving that the meeting and confession took place prior to Bodman's arrests.

"The agent that claimed to have broken the case, Jim Bodman, talks about all these clandestine meetings at the back of motels," Williams chuckled, "but it's a bit anticlimactic when the guy previously walked into the Mobile Police Department and confessed."

At the bond hearing in June 1983, a sunglasses-wearing Henry Hays confidently told the judge that he had "a good job" at the service station and that he wanted to "try to get this thing settled" as soon as possible so he could return to it.

Though only seventeen at the time of the murder, Tiger Knowles agreed to be tried as an adult, admitting his guilt privately in Judge W. Brevard Hand's chamber.

"As part of Knowles' plea bargain, he is expected to testify against Hays," reported the *Mobile Register.*

Just two days after his arrest, a gag order was placed on Henry Hays for fear the Klan might begin intimidating witnesses.

"The Klan knows who these witnesses is and they have no intentions whatsoever to interfere," Henry's father, Grand Titan Bennie Jack Hays, assured the courts. "You people have a job to do, and we want it done and off our backs."

A few days later, he added, "We're one of the peaceful groups within the Klan. I'm Catholic myself, and when it comes to picking on a black fellow—well, God created them, too."

Bennie Jack Hays maintained his pious position, assuring all who would listen that as a Catholic, he would never suggest that Klansmen harm blacks, that he was actually friends and business associates with many of them.

Henry Hays seconded his father's position, assuring police that although he was a Klansmen, he was sickened by viewing Michael Donald's body wavering a few inches above the ground on the morning on March 21, 1981.

But his words fell on deaf ears.

On Wednesday, June 22, 1983, Henry Hays was indicted for murder.

"This should be proof-positive that the city and the state, in addition to the federal government, are committed to preserving and protecting the rights of all citizens," said District Attorney Chris Galanos.

On Friday, July 8, 1983, Henry Hays pleaded not guilty to capital murder charges, smiling at his father during the proceedings.

As his son was led away in chains, Bennie Jack assured reporters that Henry was "holding up good" and maintained his innocence. Both father and son had been quite forthright in admitting their Klan affiliation, and after Henry's arrest, Bennie Jack continued his public relations work, though he suddenly began sounding more like Martin Luther King Jr. than the Grand Titan of the United Klans of America.

"A radical group?" he asked innocently. "We are not. No way. Who am I to say I'm superior over any people? We've got to live here together."

On Tuesday, December 6, 1983, Henry Hays—"dressed in pinkish slacks and a suit vest" according to the *Mobile Register*—stepped into the Mobile courtroom amid tight security. Walk-through metal detectors had been set up for the trial, and the courtroom soon filled with over forty-five people, including Michael Donald's mother, Beulah Mae, and various relatives.

Henry Hays spent much of the first morning scribbling on a piece of paper and only half listening to the proceedings taking place around him.

Acting District Attorney Tom Harrison promised the court to bring Tiger Knowles to testify against Henry Hays, to which Hays's attorney, M. A. Marsal, scoffed that Tiger was "the biggest liar that ever came down the track."

"It reeks of the worst corruption ever brought to a jury in Mobile County," Marsal told the court. "You'll find that Tiger is the culprit in this case. He's sold his testimony for a reward."

The attorney went on to discredit the witness, reminding the jury of the wildly varied interpretations that Tiger had already told the court, including the tale that Tiger and Henry had beaten Michael as an act of self-defense only after Michael had "swung a limb at Tiger." Knowles had also claimed that he and Henry had considered driving Michael Donald to the hospital directly following the beating.

After eroding Knowles's credibility to the best of his ability, Marsal turned to the jury and said, "You'll find that the testimony of Tiger is not worthy of your belief."

But perhaps Hays's legal defense was simply upset that they hadn't turned first.

"If Henry Hays had cut a deal instead of 'Tiger,' then he may have been the star witness, not the defendant facing the death penalty," Dees writes in his memoir, *A Season for Justice*. "Knowles had simply beaten his friend to the punch."

James "Tiger" Knowles earned his nickname on the day he was born. Knowles's father hefted his thirteen-pound son into his arms and immediately bestowed upon him what he believed to be a fitting nickname—Tiger. On Wednesday, December 7, 1983—the day Knowles testified to the Mobile courtroom—the *Mobile Register* made note of his heft, describing him as a "chunky man with long sideburns and a mustache." He was also described as having "a ninth grade education." After taking his place on the stand, he elaborated on the details of the night of March 20, 1981, causing Henry Hays to turn "pinkish-red" during the graphic testimony.

Throughout the questioning, Knowles recounted the conversations that he, Henry, and Bennie Jack shared in the days leading up to the murder.

"We discussed what people would think if they found a nigger hanging in Mobile County," Knowles explained plainly. Then, he offered information regarding procuring the nylon rope from Frank Cox's mother's home as well as the gun at Johnny Matthew Jones's trailer.

In grisly detail, Knowles re-created the murder—mashing boots into Michael's face, tugging ropes, reaching for a utility knife. He explained how Henry later showed Frank Cox the body in the trunk of the Buick Wildcat, how he and Henry hoisted Michael Donald into the camphor tree, and how one could see the corpse dangling while standing on Henry's porch "if you strained real hard."

However, Henry Hays's defense attorney, M. A. Marsal, told a different story, noting that Henry was playing cards when Tiger "came to the apartment with Donald's body in the back of his pickup truck."

Tiger denied the accusation, claiming that while his truck had been used to transport the burning cross in the early morning hours that night, the Buick Wildcat had held Michael's body, as forensics evidence would later prove.

The courtroom recessed, returning the following day for new testimony by Mobile County Coroner LeRoy Riddick. Dr. Riddick testified that the classic hangman's noose "was pulled so tightly it left a broken bone and gaping gash in [Donald's] neck." Riddick concluded that Michael Donald's death "was caused by strangulation," that he had not died during the hanging itself, but prior to it, when the noose constricted around his neck while lying in the clearing in Baldwin County.

The clinical nature of Riddick's autopsy report stripped Michael Donald of all human presence.

While the autopsy was performed on March 21, the report was completed ten days after Michael's death, with Riddick describing Michael as an "unembalmed black male measuring 5 feet 10 inches, weighing an estimated 160 to 170 pounds, and appearing somewhere between the age of 16 and 17" (though he was actually nineteen). He also noted that the victim has endured "multiple injuries." The next seven pages of the report painstakingly detail every cut, abrasion, swelling, hemorrhage, and lesion on Michael's body at the time of his death.

Michael's eyes were said to be "swelling in both periorbital regions" while his nose was filled with "bloodtinged fluid."

"There is a rope ligature around the upper portion of the neck at the confluence of the mandible of the submandibular region in the neck," Riddick continued before detailing the "lacerations of the scalp," the swollen "orbital region," the abrasion "over the bridge of the nose."

Riddick's autopsy report offered a unique account of the murder, allowing Michael's body to speak in its own defense.

Riddick wrote: "Internally within the scalp there is an extensive amount of hemorrhage on the left side from the left frontal region."

And we see: Henry Hays and Tiger Knowles beating him with tree limbs.

Riddick wrote: "On the right anterior lateral surface of the neck just to the right of the prominence of the thyroid cartilage there are 2½ inch long by ¾ inch wide gaping incised wound."

And we see: Henry Hays reaching for his knife.

But Riddick dedicated the most time describing the injuries to Michael's neck. "The ligature is composed of ⅜ of an inch three stranded synthetic fiber rope. On the left side just beneath the pinna of the left ear the rope is knotted into a classic hangman's knot, consisting of coils of the rope with 13 loops around the coils."

During the appeals process, when asked if the number thirteen had any significance, Tiger Knowles replied, "I have always been told that that's . . . when someone was to be hanged that that's the number of laps that was suppose to be on there."

Thirteen.

Thirteen loops killed Michael Donald.

Of course, others might argue that racism killed Michael Donald, or madness, but it was the loops as well. It was the rope and the men who wielded it, tying knots with a surgeon's precision.

A utility knife did not kill him, or a tree limb, or the hanging itself.

Michael Donald died because Henry Hays pressed his boot to the young man's face, because he and Tiger Knowles took turns tugging the rope, pulling so tightly that the bones fractured in Michael's neck.

Riddick was left to detail all that remained.

Michael's brain, "a dusky red-gray," weighing in at 1300 grams.

Michael's heart, 350 grams.

Lungs: 750 grams.

Liver: 1700 grams.

Kidneys: 250 grams.

A congested pancreas.

Two hundred milliliters of stained fluid in his stomach.

Ten milliliters of bile in his gall bladder.

A small amount of urine in his bladder.

Dr. Riddick weighed him and examined him before piecing him back together.

All of which led Riddick to conclude that Michael Donald died of "asphyxia due to strangulation."

The manner of death: Homicide.

Twenty-five years later, on the eve of his retirement, Dr. LeRoy Riddick sat down with the *Mobile Register* to discuss his twenty-seven-year career with the Alabama Department of Forensic Sciences.

Of all the bodies he examined, Riddick noted that Michael's was "among [the] most dramatic he investigated."

"I arrived at the scene a little after 6 o'clock in the morning," he recounted. "I mean, that was a striking scene. I think that what I said to myself is, 'This is a very important case; take your time.'"

Much like Police Chief Wilbur Williams, Riddick, too, recalled the pressure he felt from local leaders to gather as much evidence as possible that might lead to a speedy conviction.

However, Riddick also noted that after twenty-seven years of work he had learned not to allow emotions to "override the basic objectivity which you are supposed to have."

The highly clinical, highly professional autopsy report that he completed in the Michael Donald case is a testament to his objectivity.

In a recent phone interview, Riddick described his role upon arriving on Herndon Avenue on that early spring morning.

"Well, it's all preliminary at the scene," he explained, "so I checked for what injuries were present, made all the observations I could to determine the interval from the time he died until the time he was found. He was in a striking position because of the rigor mortis, indicating to me that he had died somewhere else and had been hung from a tree rather than being hanged."

He recalled the autopsy as well, walking downstairs to the basement of the University of South Alabama Medical Center—"a small but adequate room"—where he, an assistant, and two police officers set to work securing additional evidence.

"There was the usual procedure of taking photographs of the body," Riddick recalled, "and then we removed the clothing and documented it all with diagrams and photographs, notes."

When asked if he was the one to remove the rope from Michael's neck, he replied, "Oh yes. I remember it all. It was a classic hangman's noose, thirteen coils, yellow . . . I don't know if it was nylon but I remember it was yellow. And as I was doing it, I remember thinking this was probably the most important case I'd ever do."

After four hours of deliberation, on Saturday, December 10, 1983, the jury found Henry Hays guilty of capital murder.

The jury consisted of ten women and two men, eleven of whom were white.

The racial makeup of Henry Hays's jury was nearly opposite that of Josephus Anderson's.

Prior to receiving his sentence, Hays marched dutifully to the stand one last time, tears streaming, and stated that he had never inflicted physical injury on anyone.

The jury ignored him and, after only twenty-six minutes of further deliberation, recommended life in prison without parole.

Opal Hays, Henry's mother, turned to the jury, pleading, "I'm his mother. Think about me, him and his family."

Beulah Mae Donald, who was situated on the opposite side of the courtroom, could have made a similar plea on Michael's behalf, though she remained quiet.

The Donald family hastily removed themselves from the courtroom while the Hays family lingered.

In a rare display of affection directed toward his son, at the end of the trial, Bennie Jack said simply, "[Henry's] very dear to me. This is from the heart—I hope each and every one of them [jurors] can live with themselves."

While escorted from the courtroom by Klansmen, Bennie Jack reportedly assured the court that he was "accepting this like a man," promising that "due to this verdict you will not see from the Klan any destruction of property. We're going home with this like men and women."

Yet not everyone was so understanding.

Distraught by the outcome, Henry Hays's lawyer urged the jury to consider life in prison. "Life without parole is 50 times more punishment than death," Hays's lawyer argued, though Acting District Attorney Tom Harrison disagreed.

"There's only one fit punishment for [Michael Donald's murder]," Harrison observed, foreshadowing future events. "It's not life without parole."

In February 1984, Judge Braxton Kittrell Jr. broke Alabama precedent by ignoring his jury's recommendation of sentencing Henry Hays to life without parole, and instead, condemned Hays to die by electric chair. It was a shocking display of strong-armed justice, Kittrell showing no mercy to the young convicted murderer.

District Attorney Chris Galanos said there was a "one in a million" chance that the sentence would hold up throughout the appeals process, but that if "anybody deserves it, Hays does."

To make matters worse, Bennie Jack and his wife, Opal—who had hired their son a high-priced defense attorney they could not afford—were themselves arrested for insurance fraud just months later. The lawyer fees had added up, and with no means to pay, Bennie Jack—who had an unsubstantiated history of arson (including Henry's apartment on Herndon Avenue the year prior)—set their Gunn Road house ablaze, claiming $50,000 in damages from Allstate Insurance.

Court hearings continued to haunt the Hays family, returning like an unwanted specter soon after the criminal trial when the Southern Poverty Law Center launched a civil suit on behalf of Michael's mother, Beulah Mae.

While the criminal trial had successfully convicted Henry Hays of capital murder and Tiger Knowles of a federal civil rights charge, the Donald family had yet to sue for damages.

The civil suit launched by Morris Dees and the Southern Poverty Law Center would forever alter the course of legal precedent in regards to racial violence. Yet prior to the civil suit launched on behalf of Beulah Mae Donald, the SPLC's reputation was already well established. By the early 1980s they'd already led successful suit against individuals from the Knights of the Ku Klux Klan who had brutally attacked civil rights marchers in Decatur, Alabama, in 1979, as well as the Carolina Knights of the Ku Klux Klan—particularly Grand Dragon Glenn Miller—preventing them from holding paramilitary training aimed at blacks. What made the Donald suit unique was that it didn't simply go after Henry Hays and Tiger Knowles, but instead, quite ambitiously expanded the defendants to include the entirety of the United Klans of America organization, its Grand Wizard, Robert Shelton, the Mobile Klavern, the Alabama Rescue Service, Bennie Jack Hays,

Henry Hays, and Tiger Knowles, as well as an assortment of other known Klansmen. Everyone connected to the UKA suddenly found himself on trial. The SPLC had sounded the call for a war against hate.

After the initial days of the trial, while driving home to Montgomery, SPLC lawyers Morris Dees and Bill Stanton began discussing the case. In his memoir, *A Season for Justice*, Dees, along with coauthor Steve Fiffer, explain the SPLC strategy of putting the United Klans of America organization on trial, rather than simply the murderers.

"Tiger Knowles and Henry Hays had not acted merely as individuals," writes Dees. "This was a classic Klan murder down to the thirteen knots on the hangman's noose."

During the car ride, Dees asked Stanton, "Why can't we sue the Klan like you'd sue any corporation liable for the acts of its agents?"

Soon after their conversation, they would try.

In March 1986—three years after Henry Hays's conviction—FBI files from the Civil Rights Division indicated a recommendation to close the Donald case, citing a difficulty in building a conspiracy charge against the United Klans of America organization.

"We cannot simply show conspiracy to burn a cross, hang a black, or the act of burning a cross, to convict," the report concluded. "The conspiracy charge requires a specific intent to intimidate jurors to influence black defendants' verdicts."

But the Southern Poverty Law Center disagreed, and in June 1984, on behalf of Beulah Mae Donald, Morris Dees and the SPLC filed for $10 million in damages from the United Klans of America, Inc., a sum fully capable of forcing the Klan into financial ruin.

ELEVENTH LOOP
A VERDICT

Mobile, February 1987

He was soaked down in blood.

By February 1987, the civil trial was in full swing.

Morris Dees entered the Mobile courtroom, offering his opening statement to the jury, explaining the case in its simplest terms.

"This case started, actually, in Birmingham, Alabama. A murder took place up there, [perpetrated by] a black man named Josephus Anderson. It's got nothing to do with this case or this Klan. But that's how this case got started. He killed a police officer [Sergeant Gene Ballard], or so he was charged with—and he's later been convicted of that—but he killed a police officer in a pretty gruesome manner. And apparently that caught the attention of the Klan."

Dees went on to explain that Anderson's jury consisted of "11 blacks and 1 white. And the Klan expected them to find him not guilty when he was being tried."

"You're going to hear Mr. Knowles get on the stand and testify about what they did to this young man [Michael Donald]," Dees continued. "But first they had a reason to do it. And their reason just wasn't revenge. They wanted to send a message to black people in the State of Alabama that if blacks were going to sit on a jury and judge white people—cases where black people are charged with killing white people, they better watch out if they didn't rule right, because this Klan group has got a goal. And that goal is white supremacy."

Dees claimed that the murderers "all knew what they were doing. They had a plan and they did it."

He continued:

Now, they hung that body up there [on Herndon Avenue]. Daylight came. It was almost like Christmas. You will see. Waiting for daylight to come to go look under the tree. Somebody found the body and started screaming in the neighborhood, an old man going to get his early morning paper, and when he did, he knocked on the door of Mr. Henry Hays, in the house that Mr. Henry Hays lived in, knocked on the door and said: There's a body hanging out there. And do you know what? Do you know what Henry Hays did? He got on the telephone. He didn't dial 911. He already had the number written down. Channel 5 Television. Television cameras, I believe, beat the police to the scene. And he called his daddy down in Theodore—and it's a long ways down there—and he got there before the police did, or about the time.

Dees's eloquence painted a vivid picture to the jury, and when it was Bennie Jack Hays's turn to speak on his son's behalf, he knew he was outmatched.

Ladies and gentleman, I'm B. J. Hays. I was the Titan of this Klavern at the time. And I want to tell you the truth from my point and what I feel about other people that has been named here. I cannot build you up a story like Mr. Dees has built, because I'm just not qualified for it. But I can tell you the truth, what I actually know . . . And all of this stuff here Mr. Dees has come up with I have heard, I have never in my life heard anybody planning or talking about hanging or hurting anyone. And as far as the Klan, that is absolutely a no-no to even allow that to be discussed in a Klavern or in a meeting or anywhere in presence. We don't know—we don't want it. Because it's radical, it's stupid. And everything that happened to the fellow was one of the awfulest things I ever saw. And nobody being a decent human being could be proud of that I don't care who he is.

Bennie Jack recounted the events of that morning, how his son Henry had called him and told him to come over to Herndon Avenue.

"And so I did go over there," Bennie Jack explained to the courtroom. "And what it looked like actually up close, I have no idea. But nobody could have been proud of it."

After acknowledging that Donald's body had been publicly displayed just feet from his son's apartment, Bennie Jack Hays continued:

"A man would be—or women would be—a totally—nut to hang a body on his front doorstep . . . There's no way he would do it. If he did it, he would be in [secrecy], or she."

Yet Bennie Jack Hays's assessment assumed that logic had played some role in Donald's murder, which couldn't have been farther from the truth.

Later that day, Dees placed Grand Wizard Robert Shelton on the stand.

Shelton's Klan affiliation began in the 1950s, and he soon rose through the ranks to become the leader of the United Klans of America during its most violent years. He is often credited as one of the masterminds behind the bombing of the Freedom Rider busses in Anniston, Alabama, in 1961 as well as Birmingham's Sixteenth Street Baptist Church bombing, which left four little girls dead just two years later. He organized various splinter groups into one massive conglomerate of hate—the United Klans of America.

On Christmas Eve, 1969, a female reporter visited Shelton for a taped interview. Shelton had recently been released from prison—he'd served a year for refusing to hand over Klan roll sheets to HUAC officials—and appeared anxious to discuss his radical beliefs and spread word of his return.

He explained to the reporter that while Southerners were often criticized for their role in slavery, that it was actually "the greatest thing that ever happened to the Negro race of people" because it "brought them from the flesh eaten tribes in Africa . . . to this country and put them into a culture of civilization."

He continued: "But you cannot put a race of people that have only been out of the dense jungle of Africa for a span of 300 years and throw them immediately into a cultured civilization that's existed for 3,000 years."

He believed that desegregation was "bringing the white race down" and predicted an "open and violent bloody revolution" if the program was not reversed—a prediction he himself would help make true.

When placed on the stand in February 1987, Shelton was asked to examine a 1979 copy of the *Fiery Cross,* the Klan's newsletter.

Dees handed Shelton the newsletter, asking him to describe the cartoon on the front.

"It's a picture of an individual looking out," Shelton explained. "Apparently it's a white man."

"Okay. And what does it say?"

"[It says], 'It's terrible the way blacks are being treated. All whites should work to give the blacks what they deserve.' It says turn page, with an arrow."

"What do you see on the other page?"

Shelton turned the page, continuing.

"And it is a black with a rope on it . . . I was told it was used as a fill-in, for space."

However, the so-called "fill-in" proved damning to the Klan's case.

Dees brought the *Fiery Cross* newsletter into evidence in an attempt to implicate the Klan corporation with the murder of Michael Donald. If the Klan newsletter implied that Klan members were to lynch blacks, then perhaps the corporation could be held liable for the actions of Henry Hays and Tiger Knowles.

After days of testimony, the picture proved to be the deathblow for the United Klans of America.

One picture, one space filler, and yet it proved the link.

Soon after, Tiger Knowles returned to the stand, relaying the events of March 20, 1981, once more, returning the jury to the small, dark clearing in Baldwin County. He'd told the story several times before (to varying degrees of truth), though perhaps he rendered it most fully during the appeals process of 1983:

After we'd gotten to Baldwin County it was a wooded area. The automobile was pulled in towards the woods away from the road. Henry Hays and myself and Donald got out—in which sequence I can't recall—but I did get out before Donald, I do remember that much. Donald got out on the passenger side right after I did, of the automobile. When he got out he was standing to the right rear wheel of the automobile and he kept shaking his head . . . and saying, 'you know, please don't kill me and let me go.' And the Defendant and myself kept saying calm down, nothing's going to happen to you. And then Donald, it was like he was a crazed madman all of a sudden . . . I had the gun in my hand and Donald jumped me and I fell to the ground and Donald was . . . wasn't totally on top of me and Hays was kind of on Donald. So we were all three piled up. The pistol . . . went off one time. No one was hit. The gun was lost in the struggle. After the gun had gone off Donald . . . there was a utility knife, a razor knife."

After a brief interjection, he continued:

"[The knife] was on the ground and the Defendant and Donald and myself all three of us got aholdt [sic] of it and Donald kept saying, 'If you'll let me up I'll cut you. I'll cut,'" Tiger explained.

And during that struggle somehow or another—he didn't get aholdt of the knife . . . Henry Hays went to the automobile and got the hangman's noose and the both of us, Henry Hays and myself, managed to get it around Donald's neck. After we had done this Henry Hays had got aholdt of the rope and kind of run it, run the rope . . . started pulling on the rope and I got this limb that Donald had had and I started hitting Donald with it. And in the process of me hitting Donald and Hays pulling on the rope Donald would go to his . . . he would get up to his knees and then he would almost fall back down. And eventually after just a few short moments he managed to get to his feet and was kind of bent over and Hays was pulling the rope and I was still hitting him with the limb that I had picked up that Donald had had. Hays' hand or something had started hurting him. I don't recall exactly what it was but something prompted us to just switch places. I got to the end of the rope where Hays was and Hays got the club, the limb, and started hitting Donald. And just moments later Donald just fell face flat on the ground.

He continued:

Afterwards, after that the trunk of the automobile was open. Who opened it, I can't recall. Henry Hays and myself put the body of Michael Donald in the trunk of the automobile and afterwards, after he was laid in the trunk, he was laid on his back, Donald was in the trunk of the automobile. And Henry Hays had the utility knife that we . . . earlier in the struggle, it was found earlier in the struggle between the three of us. And I asked Hays, the Defendant, I said, "Do you think he's dead?" which both of us had assumed that he was. And he said, "I don't know but I'm going to make sure," and he cut Donald's throat three times.

During the civil trial, the prosecutor asked Tiger about the positioning of the rope, the specifics of the strangulation.

"So [Henry] put all his weight on it with his boot, his foot up against his head?" the prosecutor inquired.

"Yes. Well, he was standing—he was actually on his head."

"On his head?"

"Not at an angle."

"So in other words, he was standing with his foot right down on his head?"

"Yes."

"And pulling straight up with the rope?"

"Yes, sir."

"Getting as tight as he could get?"

"Yes, sir."

According to Tiger's 1983 testimony, directly following the murder, he and Henry brushed the dirt off one another, retrieved the gun, and then attempted to cover their tracks the best they could before hanging the body in the tree on nearby Herndon Avenue.

After describing the murder, Dees handed Tiger the 1979 issue of the *Fiery Cross,* pointed to the cartoon, and asked:

"Now when you saw this piece of information, how did you interpret that coming from Robert Shelton, editor in chief, as a Klan official?"

"That that's what blacks deserved," Tiger explained, "to be hung, and that we should go out and, since this was a publication of the Klan telling us what we should do and telling the Klan's ways and beliefs, that's what we should do, go out and hang people, black people."

Though asked to testify, Beulah Mae Donald declined.

Instead, Vanessa Wyatt—Michael's niece, the one who'd given him the dollar for the cigarettes—testified on the family's behalf.

She described how, after watching a basketball game with two of his brothers, Michael had borrowed a dollar for the cigarettes.

"When did you next see him?" asked lawyer Michael Figures.

She learned forward, responding carefully.

"At the wake."

Throughout the trial, Tiger Knowles's testimony would prove devastating to the Klan.

During the 1983 appeals process, Knowles claimed that he and Henry Hays returned to Herndon Avenue and removed Michael's body from the trunk. He described laying the body between the car and the hedges.

"A car was coming by so we didn't have much movement, we just stood there. After the car had passed Henry Hays and myself [took] the body of Michael Donald across Herndon Avenue . . . and we hang it in the tree. At first I was having trouble throwing the rope over the limb so Henry Hays threw the rope over the limb and I lifted the body of Michael Donald and Hays pulled on the rope and between the two of us we finally got the rope tied."

The pair snuck back inside the apartment, and Tiger noted that it was "the last togetherness that Hays and I had before the next morning, before daylight that morning when the body was found."

That night, after Henry and Denise Hays went to sleep, Knowles confirmed that he, Teddy Kyzar, and a non-Klansmen, neighbor David Kene, all left the Hays's apartment.

"The three of us walked out to the porch, the front porch, and you could see the body of Michael Donald if you strained real hard," Knowles explained. "After just a few moments Teddy Kyzar kind of punched me and said, 'Good job, Tiger,' and it shocked me because no one was suppose to of known about it, anything that happened other than Henry Hays and myself."

At the civil trial, when asked to describe the punch, Tiger said, "Well, just, you know, kind of like you would if you were in a sporting event and you were playing ball or something and you hit a home run or something and they punch you and say, you know: Good job, Tiger."

Fellow Klansmen Teddy Kyzar—who had been present at the Hays apartment on Herndon Avenue throughout the evening—offered his account of the early morning hours of March 21 as well.

"Well, when they came back about 12:30, Henry—I heard the door knob open, turning. So I looked up and Henry came in, Frank [Cox] came in, and Tiger came in third. And I saw Tiger—he had a blue-jean-type shirt that buttoned down the middle, long-sleeve, and from the end of the cuffs, both arms, down his chest and stomach he had like red stuff like it was blood. He was soaked down in blood."

During the appeals process, Kyzar noted that Tiger's shirt was so drenched it appeared as if he had "jumped in a swimming pool with a tee-shirt on," and as he removed it, "The buttons popped off in the hallway."

Kyzar continued:

We all three—myself, Henry Hays—well, all four—me, Henry, Tiger and Frank—walked out on the front porch and Tiger went around wherever Frank had his car parked and got a shirt. And while Tiger was gone, I asked Henry and Frank Cox what was they doing for Tiger to have blood on his shirt and they didn't say nothing. And a few minutes later Tiger came back and I asked again: 'What have y'all been doing for Tiger to have blood on his shirt?' And Tiger told me that they beat up a faggot and we all laughed about it. And about this time we all walked down, got off the porch and walked down the ground, around the sidewalk, the grass, and I told them the next time they do, I want in on it.

Though a Klansmen himself, according to the prosecution, Teddy Kyzar appeared to be more of a victim than an accomplice. Kyzar was highly suggestible, oftentimes doing the Klan's bidding without fully comprehending the repercussions of his actions. He also endured the most hazing from the Klan.

Kyzar recounted one particular instance in which his behavior ended in corporal punishment.

"I got the 50 lashes because I took an application on a guy, and myself and a former Klansman—he was a Klansman at that time—went down to Godfather's Lounge in Mobile. We got drunk and I wound up spending the money for the man's application. He got a hold of Bennie Hays about it and they voted on to either kick me out of the Klan for that or give me the 50 lashes. And they all voted to give me the 50 lashes."

He recounted other instances as well.

"As a matter of fact, on four different occasions I got lashes for various things. One for building a cross out of a broomstick—in a restaurant. I gotten lashes for that . . . I built it myself, the first one I ever tried building. And the second was—there was a girl named Diane Walker. She was fixing to get sworn in and become a Klansman, too, in the ladies Klan. She asked me did—did the men get whipped and punished like the women did for saying anything. I said yes. Well, she went back and said something to Bennie Hays or Bennie Hays found out about it and I got 10 lashes for that . . . And I believe there was one other time, too."

After Henry's arrest, Bennie Jack threatened Kyzar relentlessly. Kyzar had been doing odd jobs for Bennie Jack, and one day, while working on the top of a carport, Kyzar claimed, "Mr. Hays told me that I was on his payroll, that he was not telling me not to go down [to the police station] and he wasn't telling me to go down, but since I was on his payroll, if I went down there, I would be off his payroll." The investigators were continually seeking witnesses, though Teddy said Bennie Jack's bullying made it quite clear that he "better not go down there and talk."

On another occasion, while unloading a refrigerator, Bennie Jack informed Kyzar that he was "getting too heavily involved with the Klan." Kyzar claimed he was told that "if anything ever was to happen and I wind up being a fall guy for it, keep somebody from going to jail, if I kept my mouth shut and served a prison term, no matter how long it took, when I came out, my pockets would be padded with money and I wouldn't have to worry about working or any problem like that. But if I opened my mouth about anything about the Klan, that I was going to die within 8 hours, 24 hours at the most."

The threats spurred Kyzar to buy a pistol and take various precautions.

When the defense asked if, on one occasion, his fear drove him to dress in dark clothes and hide behind his couch Kyzar answered truthfully, "Yes, sir, I sure did."

Midway through the trial, Morris Dees no longer saw any reason to press charges against Kyzar. Kyzar's mental faculties were in question, and due in part to the violence he had endured by his fellow Klansmen, Dees decided to dismiss him from the case. After all, Kyzar's lighting a cross on the courthouse lawn had not killed Michael Donald.

"Your Honor, at this time we would like to move for the Court's approval to dismiss Mr. Teddy Kyzar. I do not want to state the reason on the record, but I think our case is weakest on him," Dees explained.

The judge replied, "All right. Mr. Kyzar?"

"Yes, sir?"

"Are you in agreement with that?"

"Yes, sir."

After a few moments more of discussion, the judge declared: "And so you are free to go unless one of the other defendants had planned to put you on the stand. In other words, you're out of the case . . . Mr. Kyzar, you're free to go."

Teddy Kyzar stared, dumbfounded.

"Home?" he asked weakly.

"Yes, sir," the judge replied. "Wherever you want to go."

Puzzled, Kyzar asked, "Am I supposed to come back tomorrow?"

"No. You're discharged from the case. You're dismissed."

Kyzar remained perfectly silent, the news not yet registering.

"You're no longer a defendant in this lawsuit," the judge tried again.

"Okay. Thank you, sir," he replied.

"Now, you can go," the judge repeated, and finally, after much coaxing, he did, leaving the courtroom and his fellow Klansmen behind.

On the morning of closing arguments, Dees recounted waking early, working out, and taking a walk with Richard Cohen before stepping foot into the courtroom.

In *A Season for Justice* he writes: "My personal history and the history of the South were inextricably woven into the rope with which Michael Donald had been hanged. It was time to put that rope to rest forever."

Dees's closing argument hit the jury like a wallop.

He walked over to the defendant's table, reminding the jury not to "come back with a verdict against the Klan because they have unpopular beliefs.

"In this country you have the right to have unpopular beliefs just as long as you don't turn those beliefs into violent action that interferes with somebody else's rights," he explained, "but they put a rope around Michael Donald's neck and treated him to an awful death on a dirt road in Baldwin County so that they could get out their message."

Soon after, he continued: "No amount of money can ever truly compensate Mrs. Donald for her son's death. But if you return a large verdict—a very large verdict—you will be telling Mrs. Donald and this nation that her son's life was as valuable and as precious as anyone's."

In the trial's chilling conclusion, Tiger Knowles asked to speak prior to the jury's verdict.

The judge agreed, so Tiger returned to the stand, peering out at the jury before speaking.

"I've lost my family. I've got people after me. Everything I said is true," he began. "The rope that I tied in back of Henry Hays' car in Frank's presence and that was used to kill Michael Donald is the one that Frank Cox got from his mother. I was acting as a Klansman when I done this. And I hope that people learn from my mistake. And whatever judgment you decide, I do hope you decide a judgment against me and everyone else involved. And whatever it is, it may make a hardship. But I hope you decide on it. Because you people need to understand that this can't happen."

Turning to Beulah Mae Donald, he said: "And I can't bring your son back, but I'm sorry for what happened. And God knows if I could trade places with him, I would. I can't. Whatever it takes—I have nothing. But I will have to do it. And if it takes me the rest of my life to pay it, any comfort it may bring, I hope it will. I will. I want you to understand that it is true what happened and I'm just sorry that it happened. And I hope people learn from what it cost me. Because my life has been ruined. So has Mrs. Donald's and her family's and a lot of other lives. And I do hope that you find a judgment against me and everyone involved. Because we are guilty."

In a show of extraordinary strength, Beulah Mae looked directly at her son's murderer and said simply: "I do forgive you. From the day I found out who you all was, I asked God to take care of y'all, and He has."

But John Edmond Mays, the Klan's lawyer, wasn't willing to forgive so quickly, and immediately took aim at Tiger Knowles.

"When [Tiger] testified in this case he sat in that chair and gave the details of an atrocious murder like he was off ordering a cup of coffee and a doughnut for breakfast," Mays reminded the jury. "How much emotion did you see when he took you through the details of that atrocity? How much compassion did he have during his testimony for Michael Donald's mother? As he took you through the details of that atrocious murder, how many tears did he shed on the witness stand?"

Next, he took aim at Dees's argument, claiming that the United Klans of America could not be held legally responsible for the actions of two of its members.

[Y]ou can't make an organization responsible for violent acts of its membership when it did not encourage, solicit, assist, help cover up, take any action whatsoever with reference to the act on trial. I hope . . . you won't be moved by the hard evidence in this case. Because I'll tell you this: It is the position of the United Klans of America that everyone involved in the death of Michael Donald should rot in the penitentiary. Anyone involved in the death of Michael Donald should lose everything they have in the world. The very idea of picking a human being up at random and killing him just to be killing him is absolutely repugnant to common decency and the human race in general . . . In this country we do it differently. Those of you who go out and break the law, you get put in jail. Those of you who go out and destroy property, you have to pay for it. Those of you who go out and injure people or kill people have to compensate the family. But you don't go back against the organization, not unless that organization stood up, said: Go out there and do that.

Attorney Michael Figures offered the rebuttal, winding the case down by restating the facts that had already become deeply ingrained in the jurors' minds.

Figures began:

> Michael was a nineteen-year-old boy. Nineteen years old. Going to school to be a brick mason, working at night at the *Mobile Press-Register*, who didn't do anything but play basketball over at Spring Hill [sic] Recreation Center and never got in any trouble. Watched the basketball game that night, according to Vanessa Wyatt's testimony, his niece. Went to get a pack of cigarettes, borrowed a dollar from somebody to go get a pack of cigarettes. A car approaches him. Two white males in it. In a totally black neighborhood. Was he alarmed? No. Did he wonder why they were there? No. It was a free country, free city. Go where you want to go. They beckoned him over to the car, asked for directions to some night club over there. And what does he do? He tries to help them. He's going to show them how to get there. Not concerned they are white in a black neighborhood. He wants to show them how to get there. And he gets a gun pointed in his face and is forced to the back of the car with Tiger Knowles and Henry Hays, and taken to Baldwin County and to fight and plea for his life.

Later, he continued: "Well, I submit to you that the only difference in Tiger Knowles' lying and the other lies you've heard in this courtroom, especially from Bennie Hays, is that Tiger Knowles has repented at an early age and Bennie Hays is still lying in his old age. That's the only difference."

"They wanted to send a message—all across the United States," Figures continued. "They didn't want blacks on juries trying—finding black defendants not guilty or hanging a jury up when they were charged with killing a white person. They want to intimidate white jurors who might be sitting in judgment of a black person who is accused of doing something to a white person or vice versa. Well, just by the luck of the draw, we have an all-white jury. That's sort of coincidental, isn't it? The very thing that led to all this results in what [the Klan] believe[d] they were trying to achieve."

Henry Hays and Tiger Knowles had set out to show the country that blacks had no business serving on juries, accusing them of being incapable of passing a verdict against their own race. And yet just over fifty years earlier in Tuscaloosa, many whites felt a similar sense of racial obligation, refusing to convict the allegedly corrupt sheriff's deputies who had allowed Dan Pippen Jr. and A. T. Harden to die alone in the Alabama countryside.

But any sense of racial obligation vanished in the case against the Klan.

Soon after, Figures continued: "One of [the Klansmen] suggested that it didn't make sense to kill Michael and then bring his body back and hang him across the street from the property that was owned by Henry Hays—or Bennie Hays. Of course it didn't make sense," Figures agreed. "None of it makes sense. Crime does not make sense. The mind that could conceive and execute such an act cannot be expected to act logically after it does so. There's no logic in this. There's no reason in this. There's no rhyme to it."

And later: "And oh, yes, it was Michael Donald on March 20th, 1981. But who will it be tomorrow unless you speak very loudly and very clearly to send that message throughout the country? Who will it be tomorrow . . . They may decide in another 5 years they don't like white women and come after you. The fact is we're all involved in this together."

Figures concluded by quoting from John Donne's poem "No Man Is an Island," reminding the jury that we are all at risk when hate is the enemy.

"'Each man's death diminishes me,'" he recited. "'For I am involved in mankind and therefore never seem to know for whom the bells toll.'"

They toll for Mrs. Donald right now. But one day they may toll for thee. Thank you."

Figures returned to his seat.

The jury retired soon after.

In a recent phone interview, Richard Cohen, the current president of the Southern Poverty Law Center, recounted the highly emotional state of the courtroom on that February afternoon in 1987.

"It was a historic thing," he began, "not just in retrospect, but you had the feeling of history being made at the time."

He described the defendant's table, which held a spot for Grand Wizard Robert Shelton. "He was a smooth gentleman," Cohen began before correcting himself. "Well, smooth's not the right word—he wasn't a sophisticated person, but he could be cordial—and it's interesting to see someone who was responsible for so much hate and vitriol in an effort to be cordial to people who were his enemies."

Next, he described Beulah Mae Donald sitting behind the prosecutor's table, "a very determined woman" who "knew that there was risk to her involvement in the case. She knew that the Klan did not have an enormous amount of money, but she was very, very determined not to see other mothers suffer as she had. So we had the most notorious Klan group in modern history, and this African-American grandmother with great faith in the judicial system."

Cohen paused. "Of course, we also had Tiger Knowles . . . and his testimony was grisly and gripping and . . . he addressed the jury and said it was all true. Then he turned to Mrs. Donald and kind of asked for her forgiveness. It was quite a moment. Usually trials are . . . I don't want to say mundane . . . good trials aren't mundane, they're morality plays. This was certainly a morality play."

He described the "spine-tingling" sensation as the jury left the room to decide their verdict.

The stakes were high.

After all, the Southern Poverty Law Center wasn't simply trying a case against Henry Hays. They were putting the entire United Klans of America organization on trial.

"We put into evidence [the UKA's] complicity in the Birmingham church bombings that killed those four girls, their complicity in the beating of the Freedom Riders in 1961, their complicity in the murder of Viola Liuzzo in the Selma to Montgomery march in 1965. We put in this evidence that put into context—a large historic context—what had happened to Michael Donald. Michael's death was just the latest of a long series of Klan killings."

When asked of his impressions of Tiger Knowles, Cohen hesitated.

"That's a difficult thing . . . I had mixed feelings about Knowles. On the one hand, I do believe in the power of redemption—not necessarily in the religious sense, but more in the sense that I don't think any of us is a reflection of our worst act . . . Tiger had been caught up in the hate when he was young, and he was kind of led astray by it. So I thought in some sense, in his own way," Cohen said, pausing before continuing, "he was a victim of racism and hatred, too. In that sense, I could understand . . . kind of . . . I wanted to believe in his conversion."

Another pause.

"On the other hand, there was an element of him that . . . I didn't know him personally, didn't spend time with him personally. I was not always so sure in the way that he had taken a plea . . . the plea had spared his life, while his co-defendant at the criminal trial was given the death penalty and ultimately executed. I would say I was 75 percent convinced that Tiger was a new person, but I had some residual doubt."

Later, Cohen would say he was "90 percent certain" of Tiger's conversion, though he did wonder if the conversion was an attempt at "saving his own skin."

Mobile District Attorney Chris Galanos was far less generous in his assessment of Tiger Knowles.

"I spent lots of time with Tiger Knowles," Galanos recalled, "and it was pretty clear that Tiger wanted to cut a deal from the beginning. He was transported to numerous prisons throughout the United States, and he was obviously feeding information to us on a piecemeal basis. I interviewed Tiger Knowles at least six to eight times . . . he was trying to save his own ass. He had to be reminded on numerous occasions that unless he was more forthcoming, he, too, would be facing the electric chair because the agreement between the U.S. government and Tiger was not only that he tell the truth, but that he tell the *entire* truth. And he had to be reminded rather forcefully of that on numerous occasions."

"In the beginning, I don't think he was remorseful at all," Galanos admitted. "He could talk about this murder as casually as if he were discussing an Alabama football game. I am not a clinician, but I thought he was a sociopath. He just did not have a conscience."

D.A. Investigator Bob Eddy also recalled an occasion in which he sat down with Knowles and asked him point-blank why they had hung the body so close to the Hays's apartment.

"Well, we didn't think the police would think it was a Klan case because we'd hung it so close," Tiger had replied.

It was the same logic Bennie Jack would use during his testimony; that no one was stupid enough to do that.

"He was a seventeen-year-old kid," Eddy reiterated. "Tiger was seventeen years old. I just . . . it just kind of dumbfounds me that a seventeen-year-old kid is thinking like that, but he was."

Four and a half hours later, the jury returned with its verdict.

"We, the jury, find for the plaintiff and against defendant United Klans of America . . . We fix plaintiff's damages at seven million dollars."

It was a crippling blow to the Klan—rendering the organization penniless—and the symbolism was lost on no one.

"History would show that an all-white Southern jury had held the Klan accountable after all these years," Dees and Fiffer write in *A Season for Justice*. "The healing could begin."

Dees recalled Richard Cohen passing him a note at the conclusion of the trial: "Thank you for letting me be a part of this."

While money was the cause of Sergeant Gene Ballard's death—owing to Anderson's botched bank robbery—it was the result of Michael Donald's.

"I don't need [money]," Beulah Mae reiterated in the months preceding her death. "I live day to day, like always. But there's some sad people in the world who don't have food to eat or a decent place to stay. I've been there. I know what it means to have nothing. If the Klan don't give me a penny, that's O.K. But if they do, I'm going to help a lot of people who don't have none."

Days after the jury returned the seven-million-dollar verdict, an editorial in the *Mobile Register* noted that the courts had sent "a loud, clear message that Mobilians, Alabamians, and Southerners will not tolerate the racist activities of the Klan."

While the Klan didn't have seven million dollars at their disposal, they did have one major asset: a seventy-four-hundred-square-foot building on the shores of Lake Tuscaloosa. The Klan headquarters was said to be worth $250,000 though it sold for far less.

Dees received the deed and the keys in the mail soon after, which he then turned over to Beulah Mae, who would eventually sell it and buy her first home. But the Donalds didn't become rich from the lawsuit. Michael Wilson of the *Mobile Register* reports that the Donald family received just over $50,000 from the sale, "less than 1 percent of the $7 million . . ."

"When Center staffers went to see the building, they found it barren," Dees and Fiffer write in their book. "Shelton and his aides had taken everything except a wooden plaque that hung on a wall in the lobby. 'KKK YESTERDAY TODAY AND TOMORROW,' it read."

In 1933, Tuscaloosa's racial hatred claimed the lives of Dan Pippen Jr. and A. T. Harden.

Fifty-four years later, Beulah Mae Donald commandeered hate's headquarters in the very same town.

Today, the former Klan headquarters is covered in gray siding, a few flowerpots littered beside a small fountain. It sits atop a hill on Lester Taylor Road, a twenty-minute drive from downtown Tuscaloosa. From atop the hill, you can almost make out Lake Tuscaloosa just beyond the tree line. Currently, it's a private residence, though on Thursday nights, for a $4 cover charge, all are welcome to enjoy the blue grass concerts that take place there throughout the year.

While the former Klan headquarters resides on one side of Lake Tuscaloosa, Prewitt Cemetery—one of the oldest slave cemeteries in the nation—sits on the other. It's an odd contradiction—one location for perpetuating hate and one for preserving love. Yet regardless of purpose, both locations are picturesque, hidden among the trees on quiet roads, just short walks from the water.

Undoubtedly, Lake Tuscaloosa has a sordid history with race, as does the city itself. While the 1933 lynchings of Pippen and Harden were not necessarily Klan-related, the KKK organization continued to grow throughout the late forties and early fifties. According to the *West Alabama Breeze*, the Tuscaloosa chapter of the Klan reemerged in April 1917, with the Imperial Wizard W. J. Simmons himself overseeing the fledgling club. While the 1917 papers deemed the Klan the "latest and most needed patriotic, fraternal order" of "real men," later Tuscaloosa papers would not offer it the same praise.

In late May and early June of 1949, Pulitzer Prize–winning editor Buford Boone of the *Tuscaloosa News* ran a series of Klan articles, one of which exposed the Klan for using a county building, the VFW lodge, to hold its Friday night meetings. Boone's moderate views, particularly throughout the fifties and sixties, made him quite unpopular throughout Tuscaloosa and the South. He regularly received hate mail and death threats, yet he continued on in his efforts toward peaceful integration. Most known for his coverage of African-American Autherine Lucy's admission into the University of Alabama in 1956, he was also notorious for his refusal to be intimidated by the local Klan.

Rather than praise the Klan for their efforts as had occurred under previous editorships of the *Tuscaloosa News*, Boone exposed them for what they were. He infiltrated a Klan meeting, reporting on their "dirty talk," noting that mid-meeting, one Klansman actually stood up to protest "against the manner in which sessions are conducted," informing the others that he knew some citizens refused to join because of the "indecent conversation." As the articles continued to run, Klansmen feared a traitor in their midst, noting that a "bad man in this organization can do us a lot of damage."

Nearly forty years later, at the conclusion of *Beulah Mae Donald vs. United Klans of America*, the UKA experienced this damage firsthand, their bank account running dry as a result of Tiger Knowles's confession.

Yet in the years following Boone's critical articles, the Klan's power throughout the state only intensified. In 1961, Robert Shelton became the Grand Wizard of the United Klans of America, a new group that brought the smaller factions together, concentrating their influence while simultaneously coordinating attacks. As Cohen alluded to, the UKA was accused of several violent crimes, but Shelton and the UKA made their presence known, not only through violence, but also by holding rallies throughout Alabama, including one photographed just off U.S. 82 on April 23, 1965, crosses enflamed as the masked men peered out from their eyeholes at their destruction.

Twenty-one years after the rally, early on the evening of March 20, 1981, Beulah Mae Donald remained a quiet, hardworking mother, though after her son was murdered later that evening, she became anything but quiet.

She refused to allow Michael to be "just another colored man, as they say, gone on and forgotten."

With the help of the Southern Poverty Law Center and the local and statewide divisions of the NAACP, she sued the Ku Klux Klan, eventually earning the title "the woman who beat the Klan" from various newspapers.

Michael was the youngest child, the only one still living at home, and after his murder, Beulah was shocked by the random brutality that took her son.

She died of natural causes in September 1988, a year and a half after the conclusion of the civil suit. She was pronounced dead by county coroner LeRoy Riddick—the same man who pronounced Michael dead just seven years before.

"She'll forever have a place in history as the woman who beat the Klan," Morris Dees commented upon her death. "I just think she was a brave and courageous woman whose love for her son insured that he did not die in vain."

He certainly hadn't.

Michael Donald's death cost the United Klans of America virtually every penny they had.

TWELFTH LOOP
A DATE WITH YELLOW MAMA

Holman Correctional Facility, February 1984–June 6, 1997

If I can help in the not too distant future, let me know.

Henry Hays was put to death for a dollar.

He was originally indicted for "committing murder with a rope in the course of a kidnapping," yet prosecutors realized that "murder-kidnapping was not a capital offense at the time."

They revised their strategy, returning to the dollar Donald had borrowed to buy the cigarettes.

While shoved in the backseat of the Buick Wildcat, Henry Hays and Tiger Knowles demanded Michael empty his pockets to ensure he was unarmed. In the process, a single dollar slipped out, along with his wallet.

The Grand Jury stated that since Henry Hays "feloniously [took] the said currency and wallet of the approximate aggregate value of two-dollars ($2), from Michael Donald's person," Hays could be charged with intentionally causing the death of another person.

It could be considered robbery, and the indictment changed to murder in the course of a robbery—a capital offense.

If Michael had made it to the Gulf station first and a pack of cigarettes had fallen from his pocket rather than the dollar, there is a possibility that Henry Hays may have received life without parole. But Henry Hays and Tiger Knowles abducted Michael a few minutes too early, an error that put the death penalty back in play for the prosecution.

In July 1993, Henry Hays appealed on what he described as "violations to his rights under the U.S. Constitution," claiming that changing his indictment to include robbery just hours before his trial hurt his defense. He also claimed that Tiger had changed his story too many times to be considered a credible witness.

The courts denied his appeal.

He tried again two years later, though the court remained steadfast.

"The drums start to beat a little faster right now," admitted Hays's attorney, Rick Kerger, upon realizing the appeals process was coming to its end.

When asked of his involvement in the case, Kerger explained, "About two or three years earlier they had solicited lawyers who were willing to take pro bono death penalty cases and I agreed to do that. And then at the end of October 1986, I got a phone call from the NAACP Legal Defense Education Fund . . . They said they had nothing in Ohio, but they were having trouble finding someone for a guy in Alabama. They said it was the case of a KKK who hung a young black man down in Mobile. I said, 'You're the NAACP Defense Fund?' and she said, 'We work against the death penalty no matter who it's directed against.' And that's how it started."

In 1996, in a last-ditch effort, Hays stood in front of the 11th U.S. Circuit Court of Appeals and argued, unsuccessfully, for a change of heart. This final blow forced Henry Hays to come to terms with what the state of Alabama had understood for years: The electric chair lingered just beyond Hays's horizon.

Holman Correctional Facility sits on an empty expanse of land in Atmore, Alabama, with barbed wire coiling around the fences and a guard tower hovering within view. The prison was opened in the winter of 1969, originally to house 520 inmates, though currently, the prison boasts nearly twice that number. For nearly fourteen years, Henry Hays was one of them, along with Josephus Anderson, whose deadlocked verdict in the killing of Sergeant Gene Ballard had spurred Henry Hays to act. There is no evidence that Hays and Anderson ever knew one another or made the connection between their shared fates—how one murder had spurred another, sending both Anderson and Hays to prison—yet it's worth our speculation.

Did Anderson and Hays ever cross paths during their shared years at Holman Correctional Facility? Had they ever shared a cell block? While Anderson remains in Holman to this day, he has not responded to my attempts to contact him.

In May 1997, the Alabama Supreme Court settled on Henry Hays's execution date: June 6, 1997, 12:01 a.m.

Nevertheless, Henry Hays maintained his innocence, claiming he had taken "no part in the random killing" and "unwillingly joined the United Klans of America to satisfy his father, Bennie Jack."

While his second statement was most likely true, his innocence had been disproven years prior.

Michael Wilson of the *Mobile Register,* the reporter who likely knew Henry Hays best, intimately described the thought process of a man in his final hours.

"You wrap yourself in books and television and Mountain Dews and Marlboros, and you stop thinking about grass and cars and beer, and the yellow chair of wood and leather and wire where your life will end," Wilson writes. "Suddenly, there is a day on the calendar, and nothing after it; a Thursday that will end and a Friday that will dawn without you."

On the day prior to his execution, Henry Hays publicly maintained his innocence once more, telling reporters he would die "an innocent man, trampled by ambitious prosecutors and the lies of his fellow Ku Klux Klansmen."

"You'll remember a smile we shared together," Hays told reporters, "and say, 'Maybe he didn't do it. And if he did, he wasn't such a bad guy.'"

Hays spent his last week visiting with family and writing good-bye letters. Meanwhile, Michael Donald's siblings struggled through an entire spectrum of opinions related to Hays's execution.

Michael's older brother, Stanley Donald, planned to witness the execution firsthand, telling reporters that he wanted to go in order "to see if it actually happens."

Meanwhile, Betty Wyatt, Michael's sister, believed Henry Hays had already been punished enough. "If he's got a heart, he's punished," she explained in the *Mobile Register*. "I hope he asks the Lord to have mercy on his soul."

Mary Jackson, Michael's oldest sibling, represented the opposing view of her brother Stanley, though perhaps for a similar reason.

"He should never get no electric chair," Jackson exclaimed to the press. "He should just stay there to suffer and think."

Mobile's citizens remained equally split as well, though one death penalty advocate published a letter in the *Mobile Register* stating, "If the judge wants the death penalty for a murderer, let 'Yellow Mama' [the nickname for the yellow-colored electric chair] rock and roll."

A surprising twist occurred just days before Hays's execution.

A black mechanic by the name of Claude Wims suddenly came forward, informing authorities that on the night of the murder, he and Henry Hays had been "hanging Sheetrock until after midnight."

"It's a wonderful concept," agreed Hays's attorney, Rick Kerger. "But there's absolutely no testimony, including Henry's, to indicate that was going on."

Wims disagreed, claiming that he knew about Henry Hays's Klan connections but that he was his "pal" anyway. Wilson reported that Wims "even went to a Klan meeting once, wearing a hood so no one would know."

Michael Wilson continued: "Wims' gesture, while not likely to free Hays, is indicative of the rapport Hays had with his black friends when he wasn't with the Klan."

Cecil Williams—who had driven cement trucks with Hays and later served as one of his pallbearers—recalled Henry as being "the happiest-go-lucky fellow you'd ever meet in your life." While filling up the trucks, Cecil recalled how he and Henry often "sang to get the day going, just singing and having a good time."

When Gail Cox, Henry's sister, called Cecil and asked him to assist in assembling the necessary pallbearers, Cecil reportedly grumbled, "I'd like to know where the hell the Klan's at now. He can't even get six guys together to bury him."

Henry's older brother, Raymond, was also present for the execution.

"There's more victims to this case than just the Donald family," he explained to Michael Wilson of the *Mobile Register.* "People forget that the family of the convicted, they're victims too. Michael Donald was the ultimate victim. His mom, the rest of his family. My mom was a victim because she cared as much as she did for Dad and Henry. Dad was a victim of himself. His beliefs caused him to be where he was. He was a victim of, for lack of a better term, ignorance. Henry's a victim because he never was able to stand on his own. If he's standing there guilty, he was led there."

Raymond, who joined the military and was stationed in Germany in order to distance himself from the family, vowed never to return to Alabama barring his brother's execution.

After the June sixth execution date was established, Henry called his brother.

"You said the only thing that could bring you back to Alabama is my execution," Henry reminded him. "Looks like I'm giving you an excuse to come."

Throughout his life, Henry Hays wore two hoods, one for the Klan and one as a result of his Klan actions.

In a recent interview, Attorney Rick Kerger recalled his final hours with Henry Hays.

"Essentially, Atmore's visitation area is this plastic-walled booth, probably seventy by seventy, with a bunch of metal tables fit into the floor. But in the corner there used to be a bunch of vending machines—soft drinks and chocolate—and when people would come to visit, it was a big deal for the inmates to walk the change over to those machines and make a selection. The same was true for Henry. It wasn't just that he could get some candy or some soda pop, but that he had a choice. As opposed to taking what was given him, Henry could make a selection."

He noted how death row was the only place in prison that was truly colorblind.

"The death row inmates were so tight with one another that there was never any regard to race."

The impending electric chair became the great equalizer, and as Kerger explained, "Once you got to death row, everything was fine."

At a few minutes before midnight on June 5, 1997, Henry Hays was strapped into the arms of "Yellow Mama" and a hood was placed over his head.

Prior to Henry's leaving the visitors' area, Kerger recalled a conversation they shared.

"He told me that he understood from people he talked to that when you're electrocuted, your body's contorted and your hand slams shut. And he said that if he was able, he was going to try to keep his thumb up and I was to watch for that just because that was his way of saying he'd beaten the machine. Suffice to say, he couldn't keep his thumb up when the current hit him. He was already gone."

Reporter Michael Wilson, also present at Hays's execution, described how the procedure took place.

"Witnesses watch from two separate windows," he began, "the victim's family from one, the prisoner's family from the other. When the guards raise the window shades, the man in the chair looks for the last time at faces of love and disgust."

Kerger described it similarly.

"The death chamber is probably ten by ten and there's glass in the front and glass in the side and in the front area were representatives from the prosecution and the family and the press. And Donald's brother and [brother-in-law] were outside that room, to the left. If you wanted to, I suppose, you could have craned your neck to see them. But they did an excellent job of keeping everybody separate. In a sense, I can't imagine the warden and his staff conducting it any better. There was no way it could have been done better for such a horrible thing."

The scene is difficult to envision: a human being strapped and hooded and moments away from enduring an electric current designed to stop the heart.

Yet in the days prior to his execution, Hays reportedly maintained his sense of humor.

"If I can help in the not too distant future, let me know," Henry Hays wrote to a reporter.

As a kind gesture, in late April 1997, Raymond Hays sent his brother a new pair of tennis shoes.

Henry proclaimed it a waste of money.

On his last day on earth, Henry Hays felt the cool sun in the morning hours, a chilly sixty-four degrees, though eventually temperatures rose to a comfortable seventy-six.

Yet by nightfall, temperatures became even colder.

Despite Archbishop Oscar Lipscomb's plea for clemency, Alabama Governor Fob James—who was vacationing in Canada at the time of the execution—refused to intervene on Henry Hays's behalf.

Upon hearing that the clemency had been turned down, attorney Rick Kerger and his wife hurriedly drove down from Toledo to say their good-byes to Henry.

"Unlike a lot of prisons, Henry and his family and friends had access to this whole visiting area all on their own from about 6:00 in the evening until 10:45, and they were able to talk to each other, hug each other, talk with Henry and just wander back and forth," Kerger recalled. "But the most surreal part of it was, when you're around someone you know is sick and dying, you always know it's going to happen, but you don't know when. But with an execution, everyone knew with certainly when it's going to happen; it's going to be shortly after midnight."

Kerger described how nobody wanted to look at his or her wristwatch. As he scanned around the room, Kerger noticed everyone sneaking glances at one another's watches, but nobody wanted to be caught glancing down at his or her own.

"Nobody wanted to be surprised when the time came," Kerger explained, "but nobody wanted to look like they were measuring it."

The minutes slipped by, and Hays's family and friends offered their final good-byes.

"All things considered, Henry was in good spirits," Kerger concluded. "And I think he made the whole process easier because of it."

At 12:10 a.m., 2,100 jolts of electricity pulsated through Henry Hays's body for a duration of twenty seconds. Then, a lesser voltage coursed through him for one hundred seconds, ending his life.

He was pronounced dead at 12:18 a.m.

He wore a white shirt and pants.

"Before Hays was executed he said, 'I love you,' twice," Wilson reported. "First to Stanley Donald, the brother of Hays' victim, and to Dennis Perry, Donald's brother-in-law; then to his own brother, Raymond Hays, and other supporters and ministers who also witnessed the execution."

After his final appeal fell short, a resigned Hays told reporters, "I've lived in hell for nearly 14 years. I'm looking forward to heaven."

Days before his execution, Hays lost yet another legal battle. He requested to be "spared the obligatory state autopsy," though Judge Butler denied it.

"He just didn't want to go through the mutilation of an autopsy to no good end," explained Kerger. "We all know how he's going to die."

Despite his plea, the autopsy occurred the morning after his death.

And while his actions spoke to the contrary, the autopsy report noted that Henry Hays's heart weighed ten grams more than Michael Donald's.

Henry Hays's death would go down in Alabama history.

According to Wilson, he was the "first white man to be executed for the murder of a black person in Alabama in 84 years." The last execution of that kind involved "two white outlaws" who murdered a "black cockfighting trainer on a mountain in northern Alabama" in 1911.

The outlaws were hanged from the gallows, though it was not a lynching as the punishment was decided within the court system.

Owing to his circumstances, while in prison, Henry Hays became an advocate against capital punishment, becoming actively involved in a group called Project Hope.

Having become highly attuned to the race problem, Hays believed his execution would do little to further race relations.

"If I go around there to be killed, they want to believe that tomorrow morning the sun's gonna come up, the birds are gonna be singing, all this hatred you've been carrying around for me all these years is just gonna disappear, and you're gonna wake up feeling all nice, fresh and new," Hays mocked. "It's not gonna happen. White and black children are going to be marching down the street together, singing songs of joy tomorrow because I'm gone?"

The *Mobile Register* columnist Ross Sloan agreed, noting that a state-sponsored "revenge killing" was no different than the vigilante revenge killing which Hays and Knowles wrought upon Michael Donald.

"Victims have never come back to life after their killers were executed," Sloan writes.

But Sloan was not speaking solely of Henry Hays.

In the days leading up to Henry Hays's execution, another man's life was placed in the hands of a jury. The trial for Oklahoma City bomber Timothy McVeigh was already in full swing as Hays glimpsed the world for the last time. On occasion, Hays and McVeigh shared the front page of the Mobile papers. Just a week after Hays's execution, McVeigh's verdict would be reached as well: death by injection.

"Timothy McVeigh didn't flinch, didn't even blink," reported Michael

Fleeman in the *Mobile Register*. "He just stared straight ahead when he was doomed to the same fate suffered by 168 people in the Oklahoma City bombing."

McVeigh was said to have "waved to his parents, mouthed, 'It's OK,' and then made the same wave to the jurors, nodding his head up and down."

Hays maintained a similar composure upon hearing his verdict handed down as well.

When comparing the two killers, the *Mobile Register* columnist Byron McCauley writes of the "consequences of irrational hatred."

"Hays and McVeigh have at least one thing he common," he notes. "Both committed heinous crimes and were motivated by illogical and irrational rage . . . If the horror of Hays' and McVeigh's crimes are shocking, their motivation is even more so. Hate."

However, "hate" does not seem all that shocking of a motivation. Quite to the contrary, hate appears to be a motive for many violent crimes. While McCauley never indicated having known Michael Donald personally, he did note that Michael once "walked the halls of [his] newspaper building as a mail-room employee." It was an interesting detail to include in his column, one that points to our oblivious nature to those around us until tragedy strikes. But when something does occur, our own proximity to tragedy seems to affect us as well, allowing us to feel victimized by the hate endured by another.

After psychoanalyzing McVeigh, McCauley's assessment of Hays feels overly simplified:

"Hays' hatred was of nonwhites, pure and simple."

But following his conviction, at least a few African-Americans jumped to Hays's defense, Claude Wims, in particular. Similarly, Cecil Williams recalled he and Hays singing and joking with blacks as they filled up their fuel tanks in their days driving cement trucks together.

Others might argue (as Hays's brother, Raymond, had) that Henry's supposed hatred was actually the result of his inability to please his father, that Henry's Klan affiliation was all part of an attempt to impress the man who had assigned him the nickname "Half-Assed Henry."

"He's a good kid," Raymond said of his brother. "Anyone who'd cry because a little animal was injured couldn't go out and do what they said he did. He was always coming home with a sick animal and nursing him back to health."

He went on to explain that while his brother would never "hurt anyone intentionally," he "might do it accidently."

"He's had a heck of a lot of bad luck," Raymond added. "In the wrong place at the wrong time, with the wrong person at the wrong time."

But despite Raymond's favorable assessment of his brother, he was unafraid to place a portion of the blame on the family patriarch.

"Our father has influenced our lives all along," he admitted. "He's the dominant force in the family."

The one experience shared by Michael Donald and Henry Hays was that they both faced their executioners. Michael met his on a cool Mobile night in March 1981 while Hays met his sixteen years later, strapped to Yellow Mama in the bowels of Holman Correctional.

Michael Wilson—one of only three reporters selected to witness the execution—recounted his experiences inside the viewing room, the counting down of hours to minutes to seconds, confirming what Kerger had noted, that, "in Henry's final visit Thursday everyone wore a watch, but none of the visitors looked at their own wrists, for fear Henry would notice and be reminded—as if he could forget—that he had less than two hours to live."

He described being led into the witness room and watching Henry's lips whisper, "Mike," upon recognizing the journalist.

He described Henry Hays appearing "small and pale in the big, bright, yellow chair to which he was strapped in eight places, from his wrists and biceps down to his ankles."

He described the prison commissioner standing beside the phone, waiting for the reprieve that never came.

And he described Henry's "oversized black hood," which "flutter-[ed] a little when he breathed."

Michael Wilson described how the "first shot [of electricity] kills the brain" and "a second longer one the remaining organs."

He described Henry's slumped body.

His stillness.

But he also described the aftereffects: reporters going home and calling in stories to their editors, the candlelight vigil supporters blowing out their flames.

And he described finding his way to Raymond Hays's motel room at the Best Western later that evening, watching Henry Hays's grieving brother chain-smoke as the others recounted stories of happier times, "great bursts of laughter" interrupted by "long, tearful silences."

But Henry Hays's death did not bring peace to everyone.

Following the execution, Michael's brother, Stanley Donald, met with reporters and admitted that while what he had witnessed was bad, "it was not as bad as my brother's body in the casket."

Attorney Rick Kerger, who has dedicated much of his career to fighting death penalty cases, recalled one moment, in particular, that helped him settle on where he stood on the issue of capital punishment.

Following an execution, Kerger rode back to his motel with the deputy warden. The car ride was mostly silent, except for when the deputy shook his head and said, "You know, the man we killed tonight is not the man we took in."

"That's something people don't understand," Kerger explained. "A lot of the death row inmates are young guys—in their late teens, early twenties—and they're on drugs and alcohol, out of control. But by the time they get around to executing them ten to twelve years later . . . it's [a] completely different person. By and large there's no daily use of drugs, they're more mature, they're older, they've gotten the chance to talk to other people, and they're in a controlled environment off the street. And most of them probably have a far less significant risk than people we let go every day."

He paused.

"And then there's the offshoot tragedy of death penalty work. There's a bunch of guards who go off to work that morning, kiss their families goodbye and know they're going to kill somebody that night. I don't have a real good appreciation as to how difficult that must be. I've had to be around when pets got put down and that's difficult enough, but to know you're going to be part of dressing and helping and, in one case, strapping the guy in . . . and then watching him die . . . and then helping to pick the body up. I can't imagine how difficult it must be for them."

Henry Hays's final words were not the ones worth remembering.

Far more poignant were the ones that came the Wednesday before his execution: a full confession to the prison chaplain, a black man named Reverend Bob Smith.

At Henry Hays's funeral service, Smith made the confession public.

"He said, 'You're the only one who knows this,'" Smith quoted Hays before describing the forty-minute confession Hays shared with him.

"Brother Henry, you left me with a heavy burden." Smith shook his head as he stared out at the funeral audience. Reverend Smith later explained that he made the confession public because "Hays asked that he tell Michael Donald's brother."

Henry Hays's supposed detailed, forty-minute confession perfectly aligned with Tiger Knowles's testimony except for two differences.

"Knowles testified that it was Hays who stuck his boot in Donald's face while tightening the noose around Donald's neck," Wilson reported. "Knowles also said it was Hays who later slit Donald's throat three times to make sure he was dead."

According to Smith, Henry Hays took responsibility for the murder, though he implicated Knowles for these specific transgressions.

Allegedly, Henry Hays told the reverend that "Tiger Knowles, me, and you [Smith] and God" were the only ones who knew of his role in the murder. He later added that "he'd told his father and his first defense attorney" as well.

On the day of his execution, Hays denied the confession.

Chuck Blanton, Henry Hays's old friend, said he asked Hays point blank whether he confessed to the crime. Blanton reported that Henry gave him "the strangest look and said, 'I confessed to being in the Klan and being a sinner and stuff like that,'" though he claimed his confession ended there.

"He did say he has confessed what he had to confess to man and he confessed what he had to confess to God," Blanton added.

The warden doubted the validity of Smith's claim as well, saying, "That's not right" in response to Reverend Smith's version of the meeting's arrangement.

The controversy grew, attorney Rick Kerger initially doubting the reverend's claims, too.

"What difference does it make?" the reverend asked. "The man got his soul saved. That's over with. That's Hays, me and God. I'm sorry. I'm going to stick to my guns. I'm not discussing any of it. You can believe whichever you want."

Of course, whether or not Henry Hays actually confessed makes a cataclysmic difference.

Had Hays really admitted his role in the murder to a black reverend in his final moments? Or as others suggested, did Smith lie about the confession in order to add closure and comfort to those involved?

The only clue we have is a last-minute addition to those allowed to witness the execution.

Exercising one of the few rights he had left, Henry specifically asked that Reverend Smith be present to watch him die.

Henry Hays was buried in front of thirty or forty guests in Tillman's Corner in Mobile, though even his funeral would cause controversy.

Since he'd served in the military, he was given a military burial, complete with a four-rifle salute and a flag presented to his brother, Raymond. In 1975, after getting caught with two underage girls, Henry was discharged under "other than honorable conditions," though it was later upgraded to "general under honorable conditions." While Henry had, in fact, earned his military funeral, following protocol did not assuage a growing number of rankled military men in the Mobile area.

"Why should this country allow a man who was kicked out of the Army and convicted of murder receive military honors, the same as a man who served 26 years in the service and retired with honors?" grumbled one veteran.

Despite the grumblings, Hays was laid to rest in a flag-draped casket on Saturday, June 7, 1997.

As promised, Cecil Williams managed to find enough pallbearers to carry the casket.

In the days leading up to his execution, Henry and Kerger shared a conversation in which Henry fantasized about what he would do if he ever got out of prison.

"Henry told me he was going to get a motorcycle and some black leather and a helmet and just blow off down the road," Kerger explained. "Well, the day after the execution, my wife and I were driving back to Toledo, and we got a little south of Montgomery when this motorcycle blows past us, then slows down and pulls back in front of us. And the driver's in all black, his helmet's on, and you can't make out his face. He just rode right there alongside us for about ten minutes and then rocketed off," Kerger recalled.

"And . . . I got a chill. You see, there was no reason for the man on that motorcycle to have pulled back or rocketed ahead," Kerger explained, baffled. "There was no reason. No reason at all."

THIRTEENTH LOOP
A RETELLING

Mobile, Present Day

This is a reminder to put away our prejudices, to be inclusive of everyone and to love our neighbors.

If we examine any situation closely enough, there's always some new clue worth uncovering. But history makes it too easy to search for clues in the aftermath, reading yesterday's newspapers in search of the tea leaves of tomorrow.

In the wake of tragedy, everything transforms into signs, symbols, forebodings of things to come. Logic is replaced with possibility, truths with hunches, conviction with circumstance.

Everything becomes uncanny.

Such as the coincidence that on the day the *Mobile Register* printed the story of Michael's hanging, they also printed a story related to his murderers—a Klan protest in Connecticut that had left a few Klansmen bloodied.

Or that just deeper into that section of the paper, a Kodak advertisement had the bolded phrase "Hang Them Up" (referring to print enlargements) eerily close to the story of Michael's fate.

Or that the following day, March 22, the paper reported the legend of Dead Man's Tree—a supposedly haunted lynching tree in Baldwin County, the same county where Donald was killed.

According to reporter Michael Wilson, even Police Chief Wilbur Williams was stretching the boundaries of logic, "studying the fact that March 21, 1981, was the first night in 100 years that a full moon rose over the first night of spring, and he wondered in frustration if it mattered."

As Williams can attest, when examining any story closely enough, we find ourselves grasping for connections, resorting to the alignment of stars and horoscopes for clues.

We begin substituting fiction for facts, inklings for interviews, examining crystal balls and tarot cards to fill in all the blanks.

And suddenly, even the landscape of Michael Donald's murder takes on new, personal significance.

Less than twenty-four hours after Michael Donald was murdered in Baldwin County, a tornado touched down on the scene of the murder, destroying the nearby trees and limbs.

"Golf-ball sized hail rained down . . ."

"Heavy, high winds caused widespread power outages . . ."

W. L. Patterson of the Alabama Power Company noted the many trees that had fallen onto the lines, how his employees worked deep into Saturday night as the storms raged all around them.

If the storm had hit just twenty-four hours prior, perhaps Hays and Knowles might have stayed inside the warmth of the Herndon apartment instead, played another hand of cards.

Or perhaps Michael Donald might have been the one to stay inside to grumble about his losing Jags.

All it might have taken was a gust of wind or some rain.

A ripple of thunder.

A game gone into overtime, one more second on the play clock.

There are countless scenarios in which Michael Donald never walked past the Buick Wildcat, was never asked for directions, was never held with a knife to his throat.

And yet, like all tragedies, somehow all the conditions allowed for the worst-case scenario to play out.

Only three men know what actually occurred on the night of March 20, 1981.

Two of those men are dead.

The one who remains—Tiger Knowles—has now been released from prison, though he remains unavailable for comment.

It is difficult to decipher the mystery of Tiger Knowles, whether he is a victim of "racism and hatred" as Richard Cohen suggested, or quite to the contrary, nothing more than a cold-blooded murderer.

Perhaps the answer involves a question of intent.

While Rick Kerger contends that his client Henry Hays as well as Hays's accomplice Tiger Knowles intended to harass a black man, he remains firm in his conviction that the pair had no intention of killing anybody.

Nevertheless, when Kerger asked Knowles if he agreed with that statement, Knowles answered, "No, I believe we were going to kill him," dooming his accomplice in the process.

In 1981, the year Michael Donald was found hanging from a tree, Ronald Reagan was sworn in as the fortieth president of the United States of America, Walter Cronkite retired, and Robert Redford's *Ordinary People* won the Academy Award for Best Picture. Pope John Paul II was shot. Ronald Regan was shot. Wayne Williams was charged with the Atlanta murders. And just three years later, *The Cosby Show* would become one of the most popular shows on television right around the same time Henry Hays received his sentencing.

It seems somehow inconceivable that Michael Donald was lynched the same week REO Speedwagon's "Keep On Loving You" was at the top of the pop charts; baffling that somehow, in an era of Cabbage Patch Kids, Pound Puppies, and My Little Pony, such an act could still occur.

Acid-washed jeans and parachute pants and a lynching in Mobile.

Undoubtedly, the act itself is anachronistic to the time period. Shortly after Donald's death, the Southern Organizing Committee for Economic and Social Justice released a statement claiming, "Our national clock moved back last Saturday in Mobile to the 1920s, and if concerned citizens, white as well as black, do not organize quickly to reverse the trend, we will find ourselves back in the 1870s." While one murder may not necessarily constitute a "trend," the point remains valid: lynching had long fallen out of favor as an accepted form of vigilante justice. Yet in March 1981, Henry Hays and Tiger Knowles seemed momentarily unfamiliar with the time period in which they were living. At the turn of the nineteenth century, some whites felt a great power in their ability to have an occasion to murder without impunity. Lynching seemed like a loophole, and the fact that Alabama had actually repealed its antilynching legislation sometime between 1868 and 1933 is proof enough that this loophole was meant to remain open. Hays and Knowles's error was in believing that this brazen impunity might still apply to modern times. And while from 1981 to 1983 this seemed to be the case, the murderers were eventually brought to justice.

In *A Rage for Order*, Joel Williamson manages to step inside the minds of lynching perpetrators, arguing that prior to the Montgomery Bus Boycott of 1955, Southern whites "could beat or lynch a black man," while remaining certain "that when the job was done, they could climb back up on the cloud and sail smiling and smoothly on." Williamson calls this skewed thinking "calculated insanity," noting that it was "almost as if Southerners sometimes said to themselves, 'Today I'm going to go deliberately crazy, but tomorrow I will be sane again.'"

One night thirty years ago, on a dirt road in Baldwin County, Henry Hays and Tiger Knowles seemed to believe that they, too, could leap back on their cloud to safety.

Knowles whispered, "Think he's dead?"

Reaching for his utility knife, Henry Hays answered, "I don't know but I'm gonna make sure."

Meanwhile, the University of South Alabama basketball team licked their wounds following their last second defeat against Tulsa.

That night, Beulah Mae Donald woke from a terrifying nightmare while her son swung from a camphor tree.

On Tuesday, May 16, 2006, just a few months after the twenty-fifth anniversary of Michael Donald's death, the city of Mobile renamed Herndon Avenue Michael Donald Avenue, in memory of the nineteen-year-old whose body was found hanging from the tree. The change came as a result of a push from the Donald family, as well as a city council initiative and a petition from Herndon Avenue residents.

"This is a reminder to put away our prejudices," City Councilman William Carroll announced at the ceremony, "to be inclusive of everyone and to love our neighbors."

The street sign was unveiled by Michael's brother Stanley, one hand raised victoriously in the air beside his brother's name displayed across the green street sign. Yet today, when driving down Michael Donald Avenue, a remnant of Herndon Avenue remains: a stone post with the street's former name ingrained deep, half-overgrown by weeds.

There are even fewer reminders of Sergeant Gene Ballard. A Google search brings up a single webpage, the Officer Down Memorial Page, Inc. There, his name is listed alongside the end of his watch: November 29, 1979. His biographical information is not available, nor a photo.

The incident details are matter-of-fact:

Cause of Death: Gunfire
Date of Incident: Thursday, November 29, 1979
Weapon Used: Gun, unknown type
Suspect Info: Sentenced to Life

Ballard's life is shrunk to a single paragraph, which is all that remains aside from his family's remembrances.

When asked what she thought her father would think of Michael Donald's murder, Kathy Sutton replied, "I think my father would think that it was very stupid. I think it's evil. No. It would make him sick. It would just . . . that's not the way he raised me."

Henry Hays began attending his father's Klan meetings as a teenager, marveling at the unexpected power his father possessed in front of a crowd.

"He saw his father being looked up to because of all this racial hatred," explained Hays's attorney, Rick Kerger. "You see, the Klan put most things in a context of the justice in the injustice. Before the murder of Michael Donald, a homosexual that lived in the neighborhood had propositioned a few Klansmen's children. The residents had complained to police and nothing had been done, so Henry Hays and Tiger Knowles went out and kidnapped this guy and took him out to exactly the same place they then took Michael Donald, and they stripped him naked and beat him and left him there as a lesson to stay away from the kids in the neighborhood. Henry offered that as an example of the Klan's attempt at protecting children."

Kerger continued: "In his view, he wasn't being intolerant of sexual preferences, but just looking out for the kids. I certainly don't agree with the logic, but I can understand it."

While there's no evidence that Kenneth Jones—the homosexual Hays and Knowles stripped and beat just days before Donald's murder—had, in fact, propositioned children on Herndon Avenue, at the very least he was the stand-in for the guilty party. Hays and Knowles needed a homosexual to blame and Kenneth Jones fit the bill in the same way Michael Donald fit the bill for a black man.

Kerger confirmed that Hays's rationale for the killing of Michael Donald might have followed the same skewed logic.

In their view, they weren't brutally murdering an innocent black man, they were defending an innocent white police officer.

"It makes me sick," repeated Kathy Sutton. "That would just make my father roll over in his grave."

In the Southern Commission on the Study of Lynching's 1931 report, "Lynchings and What They Mean," the commission notes that one "mental characteristic of the lyncher is his dogmatic assertion that the right person was lynched." Yet for Hays and Knowles, the "right person" needn't be the one who actually committed the crime, but rather, one that simply represented the guilty party. Much like the beating of Kenneth Jones, for Hays and Knowles, the lynching of one black man in place of another was an even exchange, regardless of Michael Donald's innocence and Josephus Anderson's guilt.

Michael was killed because he was black and because he was convenient.

Knowles acknowledged this in his 1983 testimony, stating, "[Donald] seemed like a good victim and no one was around."

While we remember the victim, the details of Michael Donald's killers are often forgotten. For instance, we forget that Tiger Knowles was only seventeen years old at the time of his crime, two years younger than Donald. Similarly, we forget that Henry Hays was a husband, as well as a father to his four-year-old daughter, Michelle. These men had jobs and families and yet still mostly fit the description of the "unattached young men and teen-age boys" that described the mob that surrounded the Tuscaloosa county jail in June 1933.

And yet despite our understanding that both of these men undoubtedly had favorite songs and favorite restaurants and hobbies, it doesn't make it any easier to humanize them.

The fact that Henry Hays drank Mountain Dew does not make him less of a killer.

Henry Hays's siblings—Raymond and Gail—viewed their brother as a pawn used to carry out their father's evil wishes, describing him as a victim of Bennie Jack's impossible expectations. Raymond, too, shared this fear of displeasing their father. Reporter Michael Wilson recounts how during Raymond's senior year of high school, he "smarted off" to his African-American teacher, and upon hearing of his recalcitrant behavior, Bennie Jack scolded his son for his poor behavior. Months later, at the end of the year ceremony, Raymond offered the same teacher a bouquet of roses and a hug on stage in front of the school and the parents.

"The first time I come to school to watch you," Bennie Jack hissed, "and I got to watch you hugging a nigger."

Reporter Michael Wilson came to the conclusion that Henry Hays's crime was simply an attempt at "[t]rying to please his father."

Rick Kerger concurred, admitting that Bennie Jack "had pretty much beaten the sensitivity, the logic, and the willingness to be somebody on his own, out of him."

"Henry was a lukewarm Klansman who'd joined because his Daddy thought he should," Kerger explained. "Once, with tears in his eyes,

Henry told me, 'The only time Daddy [Bennie Jack] ever said he was proud of me was when he came up here when I was on the row. He said he was proud of the way I was doing my time.'"

"That's what his father did to him," Kerger concluded. "Sometimes I think we had the wrong person in the chair."

The years wore differently on the men. Tiger supposedly grew thinner and more contemplative in the four years between the criminal trial and the civil suit, while Henry put on weight as his prison sentence wore on. When comparing the smug, twenty-eight-year-old sunglasses-wearing Hays alongside pictures of him fourteen years in the future, we witness a new face, his sunglasses replaced with a resigned look he could not seem to shake.

"He is . . . well, he was . . . a very articulate guy," Kerger recalled. "He was one of these individuals—and I don't mean this to sound meanly—who makes a better appearance than his IQ would indicate. I have some clients in prison who are the other way around. You might think they aren't intelligent, but they're damn intelligent, just not very articulate. Henry talked very fluently. He had pretty good persuasion powers, but didn't have a strong intellect or strong sense of character."

Despite Bennie Jack's assertion to the contrary, it is quite hard to believe that Henry Hays was just an average boy for the same reason it's hard to believe that Bennie Jack was just an average man. Bennie Jack Hays's Klan roots ran deep, though as the police began homing in on his son, he lashed out—not at the blacks—but at the "Communists."

While it's unclear if it was published, in a letter written to the *Mobile Register* Bennie Jack complained that nine people (most likely Klansmen) were being "drug into the Federal Court House of Mobile and being harassed, humiliated and threatened over something that we don't know any more about than you do. Oh Yea its suppost to be the Federal Government. I myself call it a take over by COMMUNIST."

He continues: "So I feel its High time that Decent people get together against Crime and the Federal Government, or Communism, how ever you want to look at it, Because if we don't do something about it we are going to find ourselves with no place to work or live Because the trash and Communist is taking over."

There was no threat of a Communist takeover in Mobile in the early 1980s, yet he was relying on the exact same scapegoat Tuscaloosa had employed nearly fifty years before.

The situation grew darker for the Hays family.

Michael Wilson reports that while Henry Hays was serving time in Alabama for murder, his father, Bennie Jack, was imprisoned in Missouri for his insurance fraud conviction—a scheme Bennie Jack had dreamed up to pay his son's lawyer bills. Opal Hays divided her time between visiting her son in one prison and her husband in the other. On Wednesday, May 15, 1985, just after saying good-bye to her son, she stood up to leave the visiting area and suffered a stroke that killed her.

Raymond reported his mother's death to his father in Missouri, who reacted violently, heaving his chair.

After Bennie Jack's 1987 release, Raymond admitted that his father "still messed around with the Klan."

"Signs of senility became apparent in Bennie Jack," writes Wilson. "He'd get lost driving to a Burger King five minutes away. He forgot where Henry was, asking why he never came to visit."

Bennie Jack died in Biloxi on Saturday, August 7, 1993.

His hatred died with him.

While it's difficult to comprehend the madness of murderers, the victims often fall into archetypes.

Sergeant Gene Ballard was the tough-loving father of two, the Alabama football fan, the police chaplain just days from his retirement.

And Michael Donald was the good-natured basketball-loving teen, an obedient son with dreams of building his mother a home after completing his masonry training.

While the pair never met, a web filled with hate, clouded judgment, and happenstance inextricably links them. They were the victims of circumstance in the same way that nearly fifty years prior, Vaudine Maddox was a victim of circumstance as well.

One morning, Vaudine walked through the woods with a pail of flour, though she'd never reach her destination.

One afternoon, Gene called a man over to his car just days before the Iron Bowl, though he'd never know the score.

And one night years later, Michael Donald walked toward the Gulf station, a dollar in his pocket for a pack of cigarettes he'd never buy.

It's easy to draw connections, tracing a path from Tuscaloosa to Birmingham to Mobile. From 1933 to 1979 to 1981.

However, it's far more difficult to ensure that these paths lead to some greater truth.

While the connectedness between Gene Ballard's death and Michael Donald's is inarguable, it's also skewed. It's no simple domino effect wherein one clattering tile falls into another. Instead, interfering forces come into play, linking a Birmingham bank robbery to a lynching that took place years later. Even more difficult is tracing a direct connection between Vaudine Maddox's murder and those that followed so far into the future. But perhaps the connection lies not in her murder, but in the murders of Dan Pippen Jr. and A. T. Harden—the two teenagers who were shot and killed for a crime for which they were never convicted.

Another connection between the murders of 1933 and 1981 is inherent in the youthfulness of both the victims and the perpetrators. In 1933, twenty-one-year-old Vaudine Maddox was killed, and as a result, so were fifteen-year-old Dan Pippen Jr. and eighteen-year-old A. T. Harden. In 1981, nineteen-year-old Michael Donald was killed, and as a result, so was twenty-six-year-old Henry Hays (though he would not be executed for another sixteen years).

Yet the various individual connections of these particular events are overshadowed by one greater linkage—that a cloud of evil and permissiveness has long been entwined with Southern history. After centuries of passing hatred from one generation to the next, regions of the South managed to create an environment forged in fear and unaccountability. This environment plagued the land and its people, infiltrating the air they breathed and the Southern way of life. Joel Williamson refers to this racial violence as a "controlled fury that was compartmentalized and sharply focused." Yet each lynching—be it compartmentalized in the perpetrators' minds or not—functioned only to reinforce a precedent for further atrocities. It was not until court systems began holding the mobs accountable that any changes began to occur.

The effects of these crimes reverberated outward, directly shaping Michael Donald's siblings' worldviews, while negatively impacting the young Klansmen affiliated with Klavern Unit 900 as well. Teddy Kyzar escaped with his freedom, though the psychological costs were great. Similarly, Johnny Ray Kelly's false testimony landed him two life sentences behind bars.

When looking beyond these specific instances to other landmark examples of racial violence, we see that youth continues to play a role. All nine of the Scottsboro Boys ranged between the ages of thirteen and nineteen, while Emmett Till was murdered at fourteen. In 1964, during Freedom Summer, Klansmen in Neshoba County, Mississippi, murdered twenty-one-year-old James Chaney, twenty-year-old Andrew Goodman, and twenty-four-year-old Michael Schwerner. While he survived his twenties, Mississippi's NAACP Field Secretary Medgar Evers was gunned down in his front yard at thirty-seven. Similarly, as a result of Klansmen running her vehicle off the road, Viola Liuzzo—a white woman who participated in the Selma to Montgomery March—was found dead in her car at thirty-nine.

The numbers of lives lost and squandered in the name of racial violence are incalculable, though this notion of incalculability does little to keep history from repeating itself.

How can we ever accurately judge the deeds of the past? So far removed from the events themselves, we are often forced to rely on newspaper reports and history books. And yet the accuracy of any source is suspect—no one motiveless—leaving us to pull at truths from the tangles of history, hoping that, eventually, we learn to pull the right threads.

On Saturday, October 17, 2009, I made my way to Michael Donald Avenue.

Wilbur Williams, the current police chief of Andalusia, as well as a former sergeant for the Mobile Police Department, accompanied me, along with his son, Wilbur Williams Jr., a Mobile police officer himself.

I drove onto the street from Old Shell Road, spotting the boarded-up houses on both sides. On the left-hand side of the street, midway down, a two-story apartment complex faced directly out at the camphor tree. Mattresses, couches, and other trash were piled high along the street, while onlookers stared out at us from their houses.

"This was all blocked off," Williams explained, motioning to Springhill Avenue on the far side of Michael Donald Avenue. "I drove in from this direction, and I parked the car right here," he continued, pointing to the remains of a driveway. "Now right here was where Henry Hays and the others were playing cards that night. Here's where Tiger Knowles' truck was parked. And here's where Henry had parked his Buick Wildcat."

"Over here is where the cab driver fell asleep," Williams continued, "and over here, right here near Tiger's truck, this was the only spot of blood we ever found."

He walked us ten paces across the street from where Henry and Tiger's vehicles had been parked and pointed up at the tree.

"And this is where I first saw Michael."

The tree looked as if three separate trunks had grown together. A historical marker noted the tree's significance, as well as the civil suit that followed.

"The rope was wrapped around this way," Williams recounted, running his finger along the bark. "It was tossed over this branch here, and it was tied off back here."

Wilbur Williams walked me back and forth along the street, pointing out landmarks—where Bennie Jack Hays's various properties once stood, where the crowds had gathered.

"Now Ralph Hayes and his girlfriend got into it over at the radio station, right over that way," he explained, pointing.

Eventually, we made our way there as well, re-creating the path the patrol cars covered several times on the night of the murder.

Next, we returned to our own cars, and Williams led me to where the Orange Grove housing projects once stood, where Michael Donald's sister Betty had lived.

"So Michael left from there and walked this way," Williams said, pointing down the street. "And by most accounts, he was probably picked up right around here."

We stopped at the corner of Adams and Pine to survey the grassy lots and small houses.

It wasn't difficult to envision what the location might look like at night, or what it might have looked like at night thirty years prior.

"The 7-Eleven was right down that way," Williams pointed, squinting into the noonday sun. "He was almost there."

I returned to Michael Donald Avenue once more the following morning. I woke before sunrise, driving the car down the darkened streets, eventually turning right on Old Shell Road and parking directly before the tree.

A black-and-white-spotted dog stood in front of the tree, staring up at me from his place beside the historical marker. I'd noticed the same dog the day before, though he hadn't ventured this close.

The neighborhood was empty and quiet, so I stepped from the car and made my way back toward the tree.

The dog trotted off, taking a safer position a few feet away as I pressed my palm to the tree, touched the bark, ran my hand toward the limb.

Just a few hundred yards behind the camphor tree rested Springhill Recreation Center, where Michael had clocked countless hours on the basketball courts, his shoes squeaking as he pivoted, as he passed, the echoing sound of a basketball just out of earshot.

Though I didn't know him, it's how I choose to remember him; the ball gripped tightly in his hands or weaving between his legs, his shoulder tucked low, releasing for the easy layup. Or playing defense, perhaps, cutting off the lane and forcing the ball. Shooting the three, the free throw, the short jumper. The bounce pass, the chest pass, boys toppling to the wooden floor before laughing and picking themselves back up.

Boys toppling, laughing, wiping the sweat from their brows.

Boys doubled over, hands on their knees, attempting to catch a breath.

And all the while, Michael Donald's driving down the court, his eyes square on the basket, screeching to a halt just outside the arc.

He turns, he shoots, and the ball lingers high above him, spinning, tracing an invisible path.

And Michael's waiting now, watching, standing tiptoed as he tries to will the ball.

Heartbeat in his ears, fingertips trembling, he waits and he watches, lips parted, inhaling and exhaling the thick gymnasium air.

And finally—just as he always knew it would—the ball sails silently through the open net.

His eyes close, his body relaxes, and then, he inhales again.

CONCLUSION
The Rope Unraveled

It is impossible to view the world the same after knowing Michael Donald. For the past year and a half I've returned to his city, his streets, in an attempt to better understand him. Parked my car in front of the Springhill Recreation Center just to listen to the basketballs thump.

But reminders are everywhere.

Even when driving through Tuscaloosa, my home, I often see green signs for Greensboro Avenue and am reminded of Vaudine Maddox, who, in 1933, was guilty of carrying a pail of flour, and her supposed murderers, who were guilty of being black.

While driving to Birmingham on Interstate 20-59, I am continually reminded of Dan Pippen Jr. and A. T. Harden and what occurred on a similar drive years before.

The masked mob.

Their eyeholes.

"We want those niggers."

Today, I cannot walk past an oak or a camphor tree without wondering what sordid history might be tied to those branches. I can't help envisioning the inexplicable, the gathering crowd, the excited whispers passing from lip to lip. Can't help wondering how the world may have been different if Michael Donald had never left his sister's home that night.

If only he'd been dealt some cards.

Passed on the cigarettes.

This is the price one pays for getting too close.

On Monday, June 13, 2005, ninety-one-year-old African-American James Cameron—the man who once felt the noose tightening around his neck on a warm summer night in Marion, Indiana, 1930—was wheeled to the front of the United States Senate to describe what almost proved to be the last night of his life.

"They took the rope off my neck, those hands that had been so rough and ready to kill or had already killed, they took the rope off of my neck and they allowed me to start walking and stagger back to the jail which was just a half-block away," the man recounted.

Cameron, a sixteen-year-old shoeshine boy at the time of the incident, had watched on as Tom Shipp and Abe Smith were hanged for allegedly killing a man and raping a white girl.

Cameron waited for the mob to take him next.

They didn't.

At least not entirely.

Just moments before his own impending death, an unconfirmed voice proclaimed the young man's innocence, giving him a future which would lead him to an apology on the Senate floor seventy-five years later.

The *New York Times* reports, "Although the House passed anti-lynching legislation three times in the first half of the 20th century, the Senate, controlled by Southern conservatives, repeatedly refused to do so." The *Times* continued: "despite the requests of seven presidents," the Senate had failed to "enact federal legislation to make lynching a crime."

In 2005, the apology was finally given, though even on that day, only eighty of the one hundred senators were cosponsors, leaving twenty senators suspiciously absent in the voice vote.

Years later, on Wednesday, October 28, 2009, President Barack Obama took a legislative stance against hate, signing into law the Hate Crimes Prevention Act. This act granted the Justice Department greater authority to prosecute perpetrators who committed violent crimes owing to a victim's race, color, national origin, religion, ethnicity, gender, disability, or sexual orientation.

"You understand that we must stand against crimes that are meant not only to break bones, but to break spirits—not only to inflict harm, but to instill fear," President Obama explained as he spoke to a crowded East Room.

He continued: "And that's why, through this law, we will strengthen the protections against crimes based on the color of your skin, the faith in your heart, or the place of your birth. We will finally add federal protections against crimes based on gender, disability, gender identity, or sexual orientation."

It was landmark legislation, not only acknowledging that hate crimes remained a problem in America, but also guaranteeing federal prosecution against those who perpetrated the crimes.

The crowd cheered.

We were sure, for a moment, that a new day had dawned in America.

Nearly thirty years prior, Michael Donald was hanged to send a message.

Henry Hays and Tiger Knowles displayed Michael's body just feet from the Hayses' apartment in order to prove that the Klan remained strong and that blacks should not serve on juries. Yet through their actions, the murderers also sent an unintended message: Their hatred was wholly irrational.

In her book *Our Town,* author Cynthia Carr points out that lynchings do more than send messages, they serve a symbolic purpose as well.

"These were symbolic killings," she explains, referring to the murders of Tom Shipp and Abe Smith in Marion, Indiana, in 1930, "rituals meant to drive home the point that black bodies still belonged to white people. That's why these executions were done so publicly."

While Michael Donald's murder took place in a wooded area in nearby Baldwin County, the fact that his body was transported *back* to civilization is even more troubling. And the notion that his murderers acted so recklessly in order to send their message is beyond comprehension; a brazen decision that may have cost Henry Hays his life.

Yet others argue that lynchings may have fulfilled a third purpose as well: redemption for a perceived offense. Historian Bertram Wyatt-Brown explains that one historically steeped rationale for white mobs attacking African-Americans was the belief that blacks "collectively bore total responsibility for the failure of Rebel arms." Rather than acknowledging a military defeat to the Union Army, Southern mob participants could simply shift their blame to fall squarely on a people they could still overpower with a noose clutched tightly in their hands.

Wyatt-Brown juxtaposes lynchings alongside duels, claiming that while both "were steeped in the traditions of Southern conventions of honor . . . Each had its sacred if different stylizations. One was to effect the removal of an allegedly insulting stain, the other to return the local community to its unblemished state of racial order."

Yet following the Civil War, these rationales began to blur. The insult of defeat tarnished many Southerners, and the simplest way to return their communities to "racial order" was to exert force in powerful, public displays. The tradition and decorum that often accompanied duels suddenly vanished. Guns were replaced with ropes and mobs in an attempt to wipe clean the perceived offense.

One can only speculate if Henry Hays and Tiger Knowles felt personally insulted by the Mobile jury's decision to return a "No Bill" against Josephus Anderson and if this insult is what drove them to such a heinous act. The Civil War had been over for just over one hundred and fifteen years on March 20, 1981, and perhaps tracing Hays and Knowles's action to an event that occurred generations before is a far too intellectualized interpretation of their crime.

After all, how can we ever trace a logical path through the twisted series of events that resulted in Michael Donald's death? Are we to begin with Josephus Anderson's murder of Sergeant Gene Ballard? Or many years before, on the day Vaudine Maddox walked toward Tuscaloosa with a pail of flour?

Attempting to discern a starting point to this story is, perhaps, counterproductive as well. Regardless of the events that led up to Michael Donald's murder, the result remained the same.

One evening he left for a pack of cigarettes and the next morning—as had been the case in 1933—there was, once more, "blood on the Great Seal of Alabama."

It's important to remember that Michael Donald was just one of many young African-Americans who paid a price for civil rights. There were countless others—from Emmett Till to the Little Rock Nine to those nameless men and women with their arms entwined marching toward freedom.

After a recent visit to the Ole Miss campus, I was reminded of yet another young man who endured great violence (including a bullet by a would-be assassin) in order to do his part for integration by successfully enrolling as the first African-American student at the University of Mississippi.

James Meredith, twenty-nine years old in the fall of 1962, stepped foot on the Ole Miss campus amid an angry mob of protestors. Everyone from the U.S. Marshals to the Border Patrol was called in to quell the riots, though not before two men ended up dead. Meredith attended the university for two semesters, though his legacy lingered far beyond, creating a difficult situation for the university that needed to find a way to navigate between polarizing forces.

Today, the James Meredith Monument features a life-size statue of the man facing a pillared walkway. The words "courage," "perseverance," "opportunity," and "knowledge" are framed on all sides, and a small plaque beside Meredith's foot reads simply:

"James H. Meredith, a Mississippi native of Kosciusko, stepped into the pages of history on October 1, 1962, when he opened the doors to higher education at the University of Mississippi and in the South. As a major figure in the American civil rights movement he helped lead the way to justice and equality for all people."

It is a remarkable tribute to a pioneering spirit, though just a few hundred feet away, on the opposite side of the Lyceum Circle, stands a monolith honoring the Confederate dead, "the heroes of Lafayette County whose valor and devotion made glorious many a battlefield."

The juxtaposition of the monuments in such close proximity is perhaps emblematic of the South's difficulty grappling with such conflicting emotions. *The Mind of the South* author W. J. Cash makes note of the "moral uneasiness" which he claims "haunted the Old South in regard to slavery." Yet seventy years after Cash's initial assessment, similar specters seem to remain.

For many Southerners (including the University of Mississippi), this "moral uneasiness" was a result of a single, unanswerable question:

How do we honor our past without disrespecting the present?

Tuscaloosa's racial tensions did not end in 1933, and twenty-three years later, The University of Alabama faced a problem quite similar to that at Ole Miss. On February 3, 1956, Autherine Lucy became the first African-American to attend The University of Alabama, though she remained a student for only three days. Seven years later, in 1963, James Hood and Vivian Malone attempted to cross the threshold of Foster Auditorium to enroll in classes, only to find their path blocked by Governor George Wallace in his infamous "Stand in the School-house Door." After Deputy Attorney General Nicholas Katzenbach was unable to convince Wallace to stand down, President John F. Kennedy called in the Alabama National Guard to assist. Soon after, Wallace relented, begrudgingly allowing Hood and Malone entrance into the building, paving the way for future African-American students as well.

Today, Foster Auditorium remains tucked just beyond the campus's main quad. For decades, there was little more than a plaque to commemorate Lucy, Malone, and Hood's efforts, though on November 3, 2010—nearly fifty years after Hood and Malone officially desegregated the school—the university unveiled the Autherine Lucy Clock Tower and the Malone-Hood Plaza. While the dedication was to be held in the plaza, the rain forced students, faculty, and dignitaries to crowd inside the auditorium instead.

I didn't think twice as I walked through the doorway Governor Wallace had blocked so many years before. When I mentioned this to an African-American friend sitting beside me, she, too, agreed that she hadn't given it a second thought.

"When I told my grandmother I was going to The University of Alabama, she was like, 'You can't go there! I remember when George Wallace blocked that door!'" my friend explained, chuckling. "I tried explaining to her that things had changed, that the university is different now, but all she remembered was Wallace."

As the dedication began, Autherine Lucy Foster and James Hood—the two surviving members—made their way to the stage and thanked the university and its students. Dressed in a red skirt and top, Lucy

Foster stood in front of the microphone, peered out at the crowd, and expressed exactly how she felt in nine words: "Am I in Heaven or is this still Earth?"

While much of the crowd consisted of students born long after Hood and Malone first stepped foot through the auditorium doors, this did not keep students from fully grasping the momentousness of the occasion. The crowd was electric; this becoming particularly true when the president of the Black Student Union, Coresa Hogan, made her way to the podium, turned to Autherine Lucy Foster, and in a trembling voice, made clear the effect of her predecessor's bravery: "I am here today because you were here yesterday."

In one swift gesture, The University of Alabama transformed a stuffy, old gym into a monument for progress. And perhaps the city was changed, too—ever so slightly—just enough to ensure that Dan Pippen Jr., A. T. Harden, and Honey Clark would not fade entirely into the backdrop of history.

In October 2009, President Obama, too, made history. Staring out at the audience, surrounded by Matthew Shepard's parents and James Byrd Jr.'s sisters, he concluded his speech by referencing the country's previous attempts at protecting the civil rights of its citizens.

"In April of 1968," he explained, "just one week after the assassination of Martin Luther King, as our nation mourned in grief and shuddered in anger, President Lyndon Johnson signed landmark civil rights legislation. This was the first time we enshrined into law federal protections against crimes motivated by religious or racial hatred—the law on which we build today."

He continued: "As he signed his name, at a difficult moment for our country, President Johnson said that through this law 'the bells of freedom ring out a little louder.' That is the promise of America. Over the sounds of hatred and chaos, over the din of grief and anger, we can still hear those ideals—even when they are faint, even when some would try to drown them out."

Michael Donald never set out to become a civil rights reformer. To my knowledge, he never participated in any marches for equality, nor did he endure the force of fire hoses, the jaws of German shepherds. Instead, the quiet, basketball-loving teen wanted little more than to sink the winning three-pointer, to become a mason so he could build his mother a home. Yet today, his sacrifice positions him alongside the better known names of history: Emmett Till, Rosa Parks, James Meredith, and Martin Luther King Jr.

While imprisoned in the Birmingham jail for parading without a permit, a young Martin Luther King crafted a highly specified response to the charges brought against him by local clergy.

After taking the clergymen to task, he concluded with a prophecy: "One day the South will recognize its real heroes," he wrote. "They will be James Merediths, courageously and with a majestic sense of purpose facing jeering and hostile mobs and the agonizing loneliness that characterizes the life of the pioneer . . . One day the South will know that when these disinherited children of God sat down at lunch counters they were in reality standing up for the best in the American dream."

Yet as history continues to show us, there will always be others fighting for the nightmare as well.

Sometime just before midnight on Friday, March 20, 1981, Henry F. Hays and James "Tiger" Knowles attempted to silence the bells of freedom once more.

We didn't let them.

BIBLIOGRAPHIC ESSAY

This account was based on various sources, relying heavily on newspaper reports, interviews, archival resources, and FBI files to re-create the scenes herein. I have made every effort to depict the story as accurately as possible, though certain passages were subject to educated conjecture. For example, we cannot fully comprehend Michael Donald's innermost thoughts or those of his murderers, but for the sake of the narrative, I have attempted to re-create the full experience as logically as possible with the available information.

Further, much of the dialogue was taken directly from court testimony or interviews in which the interviewee recited both halves of the conversation, and as such, is placed in quotations marks. Court transcripts were provided by the Southern Poverty Law Center. However, in a few rare instances some conversations were implied based on the examination of other sources such as witness statements. These conversations are italicized in order to differentiate.

What follows is a list of the specific sources I relied upon while crafting individual chapters. The sources are listed in approximate chronological order to correlate with the placement of the information within the chapters. If a source was employed multiple times throughout a chapter, I listed it only upon its initial use.

The numbering of the FBI Files and the page numbers therein aligns with the numbering used in the PDF version of FBI Files currently available at the University of South Alabama Archives.

Introduction: Braiding the Rope
The introduction was written with support from the following sources: "Hangman's Knot," *Wikipedia,* accessed August 14, 2009; weather data

from the National Climatic Data Center (NCDC); Ida B. Wells, "A Red
Record" in Jacqueline Jones Royster, *Southern Horrors and Other Writings: The Anti-Lynching Campaign of Ida B. Wells, 1892–1900* (Boston:
Bedford Books, 1997); Cynthia Carr, *Our Town* (New York: Crown
Publishers, 2006); James H. Madison, *A Lynching in the Heartland* (New
York: Palgrave, 2001); "Races: Lynchings Nos. 10 & 11," *Time,* August
18, 1930; "Anti-Lynching Bill," report number 1027, 66th Congress,
2nd Session, May 22, 1920; Dora Apel and Shawn Michelle Smith,
Lynching Photographs (Berkeley: The University of California Press,
2007); David Margolick, *Strange Fruit: Billie Holiday, Café Society, and
an Early Cry for Civil Rights* (Philadelphia: Running Press, 2000); James
Harmon Chadbourn, *Lynching and the Law* (Chapel Hill: The University of North Carolina Press, 1933); Glenn Feldman, "Lynching in
Alabama, 1889–1921," *Alabama Review,* 48.2 (1995): 114; Christopher
Waldrep, "War of Words: The Controversy over the Definition of
Lynching, 1899–1940," *Journal of Southern History,* 66.1 (2000): 75–
100; Joel Williamson, *A Rage for Order: Black-White Relations in the
American South Since Emancipation* (New York: Oxford University
Press, 1986); "Hearing on the Senate Judiciary Committee on the Nomination of Clarence Thomas to the Supreme Court," University of Virginia Library, 1991; Nathan Hall, *Hate Crime* (Portland: Willan Publishing, 2005); NAACP, "NAACP History: Anti-lynching Bill," 2010.

First Loop: A Pail of Flour
The first chapter was written with support from the following sources:
weather data from the National Climatic Data Center (NCDC); Clarence
Cason, *90° in the Shade* (Tuscaloosa: The University of Alabama Press,
2001); Philip Beidler, "Yankee Interloper and Native Son: Carl Carmer
and Clarence Cason, Unlikely Twins of Alabama Exposé," *Southern
Cultures,* 9.1, (2003): 18–35; Carl Carmer, *Stars Fell on Alabama* (Tuscaloosa: The University of Alabama Press, 1990); George Fort Milton,
The Plight of Tuscaloosa: Mob Murders, Community Hysteria, Official

Incompetence (Atlanta: The Commission, 1931); "Maddox Thought Murdered by 'Friend,'" *Tuscaloosa News*, June 15, 1933: 1; "Youth of 20 Who Lives Near the Crime, Taken," *Tuscaloosa News*, June 16, 1933: 1; "Mystery Maze Still Unfolds Maddox Inquiry," *Tuscaloosa News*, June 18, 1933: 1; "Negro Retracts Previous Story in Maddox Case," *Tuscaloosa News*, June 20, 1933: 1; "Jail Gathering Will Be Probed by Grand Jury," *Tuscaloosa News*, June 22, 1933: 1; "Three Arrested for Activity in Jail Gathering," *Tuscaloosa News*, June 28, 1933: 1; "No Trace Found of Third Negro Taken by Band," *Tuscaloosa News*, August 14, 1933: 1–2; "Court Appoints Counsel to Aid Negroes Defense," *Tuscaloosa News*, July 30, 1933: 1; W. J. Cash, *The Mind of the South* (New York: Vintage Books, 1941); Bertram Wyatt-Brown, *Southern Honor* (New York: Oxford University Press, 1982); Paul Peter, *8 Who Lie in the Death House* (NP: National Committee for the Defense of Political Prisoners, 1933); "Local Negroes Tell I.L.D. Stay Out of Maddox Case," *Tuscaloosa News*, July 31, 1933: 1; Robin Kelley, *Hammer and Hoe: Alabama Communists During the Great Depression* (Chapel Hill: The University of North Carolina Press, 1990); "Bloom Calls on Jewish Leaders to Curb I.L.D.," *Tuscaloosa News*, August 3, 1933: 1; James B. Sellers, *History of the University of Alabama, Volume One: 1818–1902* (Tuscaloosa: The University of Alabama Press, 1953); "I.L.D. Interference Costs State and County $1,500," *Tuscaloosa News*, August 3, 1933: 1; "Radicals Intent on Interfering in Maddox Case," *Tuscaloosa News*, August 7, 1933: 1; Chadbourn, *Lynching and the Law*; "Masked Band Seizes Maddox Case Negroes," *Tuscaloosa News*, August 13, 1933: 1; "Clark Tells Miraculous Escape from Killing," *Tuscaloosa News*, August 15, 1933: 1; "Clark Gives Sworn Statement, Mob Had 'Drop' on Deputies," *Tuscaloosa News*, August 16, 1933: 1.

Second Loop: A Challenge

The second chapter was written with support from the following sources: Milton, *The Plight of Tuscaloosa*; "Negro Is Shot by 2 Deputies," *Tus-*

caloosa News, August 14, 1933: 6; Cason, *90° in the Shade;* "Lynching by the Carpet Baggers of 1933," *Tuscaloosa News,* August 14, 1933: 4; "Blood on the Great Seal of Alabama," *Tuscaloosa News,* August 15, 1933: 4; Kelley, *Hammer and Hoe;* "Clark Tells Miraculous Escape," 1; "Clark Gives Sworn Statement," 1; "Judge Overrides 17-Day Recess in Lynching Inquiry," *Tuscaloosa News,* August 17, 1933: 1, 2; "Judge Orders Bullets to Be Taken from Body of Pippen," *Tuscaloosa News,* August 16, 1933: 1; "Both Hit in Foot by Bullet from Gun of Officer," *Tuscaloosa News,* September 6, 1933: 1; "Lynching Inquiry Resumed, 2-Day Session Is Likely," *Tuscaloosa News,* September 5, 1933: 1; "Grand Jury Recesses, Praises Judge Foster," *Tuscaloosa News,* September 7, 1933: 1; "Evidence Is Not Thought Enough for Indictment," *Tuscaloosa News,* October 2, 1933: 1; "Negro Is Lured from His Home Then Murdered," *Tuscaloosa News,* September 25, 1933: 1; Williamson, *A Rage for Order;* "Reward of $400 Posted by State in Cross Death," *Tuscaloosa News,* September 27, 1933: 1; "The Press: Mr. Graves Takes a Walk," *Time,* March 4, 1946; "Shall We Accept the Challenge?" *Tuscaloosa News,* September 27, 1933: 1; "Citizens Praise Stand of News Against Crime," *Tuscaloosa News,* September 29, 1933: 1; "Fighting the I.L.D.," *Tuscaloosa News,* October 8, 1933: 4; Gladys Ward, *Life of Ryland Randolph* (Thesis. Tuscaloosa: The University of Alabama, 1932); Sellers, *History of the University of Alabama;* Feldman, "Lynching in Alabama," 114; Chadbourn, *Lynching and the Law;* Ken Hechler, *Working with Truman: A Personal Memoir of the White House Years* (Columbia: University of Missouri Press, 1982: 45–48).

Third Loop: A Motel Swimming Pool

The third chapter was written with support from the following sources: Weather data from the National Climatic Data Center (NCDC); *Ex parte Josephus Anderson v. State of Alabama,* Court of Criminal Appeals, September 28, 1984; *Josephus R. Anderson v. State,* Court of

Criminal Appeals of Alabama, November 1, 1983; *Josephus Anderson v. State*, Court of Criminal Appeals of Alabama, April 14, 1987; interview with Kathy Sutton, August 2, 2009; Mark Winne, "Chief retires Ballard Car in His Honor," *Birmingham News*, December 5, 1979: 5A; Mark Winne, "Slain Officer: 'Good, Gentle . . . Christian," *Birmingham News*, November 30, 1979: 1A; Mark Winne and Andrew Kilpatrick, "'Oh God, I Need Help,' Dying Officer Radios," *Birmingham News*, November 20, 1979: 1A; Mark Winne, "Suspect in Policeman Murder Has Arrest Record Covering Almost All His Adult Life," *Birmingham News*, December 6, 1979: 1A, 10A; Anne Reeks, "Expert Links Bullet to Anderson's Gun," *Mobile Register*, March 20, 1981: 1B; Mark Winne, "Ballard's Accused Slayer Glares as Warrants Served at Hospital," *Birmingham News*, December, 8, 1979: 2A; Ben Nolan, "Tulsa Kills Jag Hopes, 69–68," *Mobile Register*, March 21, 1981: 1B.

Fourth Loop: A Flower in the Forest
The fourth chapter was written with support from the following sources: Winne, "Chief Retires Ballard Car in His Honor," 5A; Harold Kennedy and Mark Winne, "Mayor Pledges Vigorous Drive Against Crime in Birmingham," *Birmingham News*, November 20, 1979: 1A; "More Witnesses Offer Information on Shooting of Police Sgt. Ballard," *Birmingham News*, December 3, 1979: 5A; interview with Kathy Sutton, August 2, 2009; interview with Kalliopi Hartley, August 26, 2009; Alf Van Hoose, "Top Plow-Hand Shealy Cuts Tiger Furrow; Lifts No. 1 Bama out of Deep Hole 25–18," *Birmingham News*, December 2, 1979: C1; Mark Winne, "'Unity May Be Sergeant's Legacy,'" *Birmingham News*, December 4, 1979: 1A, 8A; *Anderson v. State*, April 14, 1987; Winne and Kilpatrick, "'Oh God, I Need Help,' Dying Officer Radios," 1A; "Face of Concern," *Birmingham News*, December 8, 1979: 2A; Winne, "Slain Officer: 'Good, Gentle . . . Christian,'" 1A; List of Alabama Peace Officers Killed in the Line of Duty, FBI Files 5: 29.

Fifth Loop: A Pack of Cigarettes

The fifth chapter was written with support from the following sources: Witness Statement dated April 21, 1981, FBI Files 2: 53; Witness Statement dated March 21, 1981, FBI Files 1: 101–2; Witness Statement dated April 21, 1981, FBI Files 2: 39; Witness Statement dated March 31, 1981, FBI Files 1: 23; Witness Statement dated April 13, 1981, FBI Files 2: 27–28; Witness Statement dated April 13, 1981, FBI Files 2: 16–17; Jesse Kornbluth, "The Woman Who Beat the Klan," *New York Times Magazine,* November 1, 1987: 626; Witness Statement dated April 13, 1981, FBI Files 2: 18–19; interview with Bob Eddy, August 20, 2009; interview with Wilbur Williams, October 12, 2009; Michael Wilson, "Michael Didn't Come Home," *Mobile Register,* June 1, 1997: 1A; Witness Statement dated April 20, 1981, FBI Files 2: 32; Witness Statement dated July 14, 1981, FBI Files 2: 273; Nolan, "Tulsa Kills Jag Hopes, 69–68," 1B; Witness Statement dated April 13, 1981, FBI Files 2: 30; Witness Statement dated April 13, 1981, FBI Files 2: 31; Witness Statement dated April 15, 1981, FBI Files 2: 139–40; Kathy Jumper, "Hays Trial Proceedings Tense," *Mobile Register,* December 9, 1983: 1B; Witness Statement dated March 31, 1981, FBI Files 1: 39–46; Witness Statement dated April 3, 1981, FBI Files 1: 233; Kathy Jumper, "Police Ask for Help in Death Probe," *Mobile Register,* March 23, 1981: 1A; "Large Crowd Attends Donald's Funeral," *Mobile Beacon,* April 4, 1981: 1.

Sixth Loop: A Domestic Disturbance

The sixth chapter was written with support from the following sources: Witness Statement dated March 31, 1981, FBI Files 2: 62–63; Witness Statement dated March 21, 1981, FBI Files 1: 227; Witness Statement dated March 24, 1981, FBI Files 1: 106; Witness Statement dated March 21, 1981, FBI Files 1: 84–86; Police Statement dated March 21, 1981, FBI Files 1: 72–73; Witness Statement dated April 20, 1981, FBI Files 2: 105; interview with Wilbur Williams, October 12, 2009; Wilson,

"Michael Didn't Come Home," 1A; Memo dated November 25–29, 1983, FBI Files 5: 13; Kathy Jumper and Eddie Menton, "3 Charged in Donald Murder," *Mobile Register,* March 26, 1981: 1A, 6A; Tom Jennings, "3 Men Remain in Custody as Slaying Motive Sought," *Mobile Register,* March 24, 1981: 1A, 6A; Witness Statement dated March 21, 1981, FBI Files 1: 28; Police Report dated March 25, 1981, FBI Files 1: 117; Anne Reeks, "Bail for 3 Men Accused in Donald Case Reduced," *Mobile Register,* May 9, 1981: 1A, 8A; Anne Reeks, "Bail Set for Men Charged in Donald Slaying," *Mobile Register,* March 28, 1981: 1; Anne Reeks, "$250,000 Bonds Are Set in Mobile Hanging Case," *Mobile Register,* March 27, 1981: 1, 4; Anne Reeks, "Alleged Perjurer in Donald Case Held," *Mobile Register,* June 12, 1981: 2B; Memo to the FBI dated June 12, 1981, FBI Files 2: 228–29; Artifact, FBI Files 2: 286; Report from LeRoy Riddick, M.D., Forensic Pathologist, Department of Forensic Sciences, March 31, 1981; Kornbluth, "The Woman Who Beat the Klan," 626; Report dated June 16, 1983, FBI Files 3: 176.

Seventh Loop: A Beating in Baldwin County

The seventh chapter was written with support from the following sources: Witness Statement dated July 13, 1983, FBI Files 3: 288–92; Report dated June 14, 1983, FBI Files 3: 210; Evidence Log dated June 16, 1983, FBI Files 3: 152; Laboratory Worksheet dated June 17, 1983, FBI Files 3: 148–51; Witness Statement dated April 13, 1981, FBI Files 2: 28; Forensic Science Paperwork, March-April 1981, FBI Files 3: 226–36; List of Items dated August 8, 1983, FBI Files 3: 239; Information dated July 22, 1983, FBI Files 3: 256–57; "Appeals Court Says Donald Murderer Should Live," *New Times,* August 5, 1985.

Eighth Loop: A Klavern in the Woods

The eighth chapter was written with support from the following sources: Witness Statement dated April 21, 1981, FBI Files 2: 53; Michael Wilson, "Cases Closed," *Mobile Register,* June 4, 1997: 1A, 14A–15A; *Beulah*

Mae Donald et al. v. United Klans of America, 1:163–64, February 10, 1987; Morris Dees and Steve Fiffer, *A Season for Justice* (New York: Charles Scribner's Sons, 1991); Kathy Jumper, "Details of Killing Related by Knowles," *Mobile Register,* December 8, 1983: 1A, 10A; Witness Statement dated July 6, 1983, FBI Files 3: 188; *Donald et al. v. United Klans of America,* 1:273, February 10, 1987; *Donald et al. v. United Klans of America,* 1:190, February 10, 1987; Jumper, "Police Ask for Help in Death Probe," 1A; interview with Rick Kerger, September 3, 2009; *Donald et al. v. United Klans of America,* 1:191, February 10, 1987; Richard Pienciak, "Caller Claims He Killed Four," *Mobile Register,* March 20, 1981: 1A, 8A; *Donald et al. v. United Klans of America,* 1:191–93, February 10, 1987; Witness Statement dated April 20, 1981, FBI Files 2: 105–6; *Henry F. Hays v. State of Alabama,* Court of Criminal Appeals of Alabama, 5:725–32, 647.

Ninth Loop: A Cross, a Dummy, a Phone Call
The ninth chapter was written with support from the following sources: interview with Bob Eddy, August 20, 2009; Witness Statements dated April 28, 1981, FBI Files 2: 179–80; *Donald et al. v. United Klans of America,* 2:380–81, February 11, 1987; Witness Statement dated March 21, 1981, FBI Files 1: 85; Witness Statement dated May 11, 1981, FBI Files 2: 241–42; "Sunrise," *Mobile Register,* March 21, 1981: 2A; interview with Chris Galanos, August 20, 2009; *Hays v. State* 4:582–83.

Tenth Loop: A Confession
The tenth chapter was written with support from the following sources: Chip Drago, "2 Held in '81 Murder," *Mobile Register,* June 17, 1983: 1A, 10A; Michael Wilson, "Bennie Jack's Klan," *Mobile Register,* June 3, 1997: 1A, 8A; interview with Wilbur Williams, October 12, 2009; Kathy Jumper, "Hays Murder Trial Opening Tuesday," *Mobile Register,* December 5, 1983: 2A; Chip Drago, "Court Places Gag Order

on Hays Charges," *Mobile Register*, June 18, 1983: 1A; "Blacks Criticize Handling of Alabama Klan Case," *New York Times*, June 20, 1983: B10; Kathy Jumper, "Hays Indicted for Donald Murder," *Mobile Register*, June 23, 1983: 1A, 8A; Kathy Jumper, "Klansman Pleads Innocent to Capital Murder Charge," *Mobile Register*, July 9, 1983: 1B; Kathy Jumper, "Hays Said Looking for a Black," *Mobile Register*, December 7, 1983: 1A, 6A; Dees and Fiffer, *A Season for Justice*; Jumper, "Details of Killing Related by Knowles," 1A, 10A; Jumper, "Hays Trial Proceedings Tense," 1B; Report from LeRoy Riddick, M.D., Forensic Pathologist, Department of Forensic Sciences, March 21, 1981; *Hays v. State*, 2:163; Ron Colquitt, "Expert in Evidence," *Mobile Register*, June 26, 2006: 1B, 3B; interview with LeRoy Riddick, August 19, 2009; Kathy Jumper, "Hays Found Guilty of Capital Murder," *Mobile Register*, December 11, 1983: 1A, 8A; "Klansman Receives Death Sentence," *Washington Post*, February 3, 1984: A20; Arthur Drago Jr., "KKK Official, Wife Charged with Fraud," *Mobile Register*, September 14, 1984: 1A, 6A; FBI Files 6, Notice to Close File dated March 19, 1986: 21–23.

Eleventh Loop: A Verdict

The eleventh chapter was written with support from the following sources: *Donald et al. v. United Klans of America*, 1:54–56, 58–61, 71–75, February 10, 1987; Marsha Tompkins, "Interview with Robert Shelton," WBAI, New York, 1969; *Donald et al. v. United Klans of America*, 1:112–13, February 10, 1987; *Hays v. State*, 2:145–49; *Donald et al. v. United Klans of America*, 1:201–22, 254, February 10, 1987; *Hays v. State*, 2:152–53; *Donald et al. v. United Klans of America*, 1:198, February 10, 1987; *Ibid.*, 2:377–79, February 11, 1987; *Hays v. Alabama*, 4:579; *Donald et al. v. United Klans of America*, 2:371, 384–88, 490–91, February 11, 1987; Dees and Fiffer, *A Season for Justice*; *Donald et al. v. United Klans of America*, 3:610–11, February 12, 1987; Kornbluth, "The Woman Who Beat the Klan," 626; *Donald et al. v.*

United Klans of America, 3:613–23, 3:628–36, February 12, 1987; interview with Richard Cohen, August 4, 2009; interview with Chris Galanos, August 20, 2009; interview with Bob Eddy, August 21, 2009; Herb Jordan, "Jury Rules Against Klansmen," *Mobile Register*, February 13, 1983: 1A, 12A; Robin Toner, "A Mother's Struggle with the Klan," *New York Times*, March 8, 1987; Kathy Jumper, "Mother Sought Reasons, Not Revenge, for Killing," *Mobile Register*, December 28, 1987: 1A, 11A; "Society Holds No Place for the Klan," *Mobile Register*, February 14, 1987: 4A; Herb Jordan, "Hearing Ordered on Klan Award," *Mobile Register*, February 13, 1987: 1A, 16A; Garry Mitchell, "Civil Rights Leaders Hail KKK Verdict," *Mobile Register*, February 14, 1987: 1A, 8A; Michael Wilson, "Jury's $7 Million Verdict Mostly a Paper Victory," *Mobile Register*, June 4, 1997: 14A; "The Ku Klux Klan Organized at Tuscaloosa," *West Alabama Breeze*, April 4, 1917: 6; Buford Boone, "KKK Mask Is Off," *Tuscaloosa News*, May 27, 1949: 1A; Buford Boone, "Klansman Hits 'Dirty' Talk at KKK Meeting," *Tuscaloosa News*, May 28, 1949: 1A; Buford Boone, "Klan Afraid of Bad Man," *Tuscaloosa News*, May 29, 1949: 1A; Buford Boone, "Klan Looks Forward to Time When It Can 'Run the Town,'" *Tuscaloosa News*, May 30, 1949: 1A; Rebecca Woodham, "Buford Boone," *Encyclopedia of Alabama*, 2008; "Beulah M. Donald, 67, Klan Foe," *New York Times*, September 20, 1988: D29.

Twelfth Loop: A Date with Yellow Mama

The twelfth chapter was written with support from the following sources: Wilson, "Cases Closed," 1A, 14A–15A; Grand Jury No. 118, Indictment, December 5, 1983, FBI Files 5: 26; Michael Wilson, "New Trial for Hays Denied," *Mobile Register*, March 7, 1995: 1B, 3B; Renee Busby, "Hearing Held on Hays Request for New Trial, Reduced Sentence," *Mobile Register*, June 23, 1989: 1D; interview with Rick Kerger, September 3, 2009; Michael Wilson, "Klanman's Death Row Appeal Rejected by Circuit Court," *Mobile Register,* June 8, 1996: 2B; "Ex-Klansman Hays Gets June 6 Execution Date," *Mobile Register,* May 2, 1997: 1A, 4A; Michael Wilson, "The Final Hours," *Mobile Register:* June 5, 1997, 1A, 18A; Sharron Fontana, "Let 'Yellow Mama' Rock and Roll Along," *Mobile Register,* June 10, 1997: 8A; Michael Wilson, "Family Members Plead for Henry Hays' Life," *Mobile Register,* June 4, 1997: 15A; Michael Wilson, "Old Friend Offers Surprise Alibi for Henry Hays," *Mobile Register,* June 4, 1997: 15A; weather data from the National Climatic Data Center (NCDC); Pamela H. Long, "Lipscomb's Plea for Hays' Life Not Unusual, Spokesman Says," *Mobile Register,* June 8, 1997: 4A; Michael Wilson, "Hays Put to Death," *Mobile Register,* June 7, 1997: 1A, 4A; Michael Wilson, "Witness to an Execution," *Mobile Register,* June 10, 1997: 1A, 4A; Henry F. Hays' Autopsy Report Alabama Department of Forensic Sciences, October 6, 1997; Ross Sloan, "In an Execution's Aftermath, Let Us Kill Capital Punishment," *Mobile Register,* June 9, 1997: 6A; Michael Fleeman, "Death for McVeigh," *Mobile Register,* June 14, 1997: 1A, 4A; Byron McCauley, "The Consequences of Irrational Hatred," *Mobile Register,* June 7, 1997: 4A; Kathy Jumper, "Hays Family Is Bound Together by Strong Ties," *Mobile Register,* February 3, 1984: 1B–2B; Michael Wilson, "Hays Made Confession to Minister," *Mobile Register,* June 8, 1997: 1A, 12A; Michael Wilson, "Warden Questions Minister's Version," *Mobile Register,* June 13, 1997: 1A, 4A; Ron Colquitt, "Hays Was Entitled to Military Burial Honors," *Mobile Register,* June 11, 1997: 1A, 4A.

Thirteenth Loop: A Retelling

The thirteenth chapter was written with support from the following sources: Peter Hawes, "Klansmen Bloodied by Opposition in Connecticut," *Mobile Register,* March 22, 1981: 16A; Buddy Smith, "Nature Factor in Eliminating Obscure Legend from Baldwin," *Mobile Register,* March 22, 1981: 4B; Michael Wilson, "Michael Didn't Come Home,"

1A, 18A, 19A; Kathy Jumper, "Rains, Hail End Fire Alert," *Mobile Register*, March 23, 1981: 1A; interview with Richard Cohen, August 4, 2009; interview with Rick Kerger, September 3, 2009; "Mobile Murder Protested as a Lynching," *Mobile Beacon*, April 11, 1981: 1; Chadbourn, *Lynching and the Law*; Williamson, *A Rage for Order*; Kornbluth, "The Woman Who Beat the Klan," 626; Nadia M. Taylor, "Street Renamed for Michael Donald," *Mobile Register*, May 17, 2006: 1B; Officer Down Memorial Page; interview with Kathy Sutton, August 2, 2009; George Fort Milton, *Lynchings and What They Mean* (Atlanta: The Commission, 1931); Jumper, "Details of Killing Related by Knowles," 1A, 10A; Michael Wilson, "Raised in Hate," *Mobile Register*, June 2, 1997: 1A, 6A; Milton, *The Plight of Tuscaloosa*; Letter to the Editor, FBI Files 3: 187; Michael Wilson, "Cases Closed," 1A, 14A–15A; interview with Wilbur Williams, October 17, 2009.

Conclusion: The Rope Unraveled

The conclusion was written with support from the following sources: Sheryl Gay Stolberg, "Senate Issues Apology over Failure on Lynching Law," *New York Times*, June 14, 2005: A15; "Remarks by the President at Reception Commemorating the Enactment of the Matthew Shepard and James Byrd, Jr. Hate Crimes Prevention Act," The White House, Washington D.C., October 28, 2009; Carr, *Our Town*; Bertram Wyatt-Brown, *The Shaping of Southern Culture* (Chapel Hill: The University of North Carolina Press, 2001); Milton, *The Plight of Tuscaloosa*; Cash, *The Mind of the South*; Martin Luther King, "Letter from a Birmingham Jail."

BIBILIOGRAPHY

Archives and Manuscripts

Anthony Blasi Papers. Hoole Library, The University of Alabama, Tuscaloosa.

Birmingham Civil Rights Institute. BCRI, Birmingham.

FBI Files 1–5. The University of South Alabama Archives, Mobile.

Hazel Eubanks Papers. Hazel Eubanks, Tuscaloosa, Alabama.

Michael Donald Collection. The University of South Alabama Archives, Mobile.

R. L. Hanvey Papers. Hoole Library, The University of Alabama, Tuscaloosa.

Trial Transcripts. Southern Poverty Law Center Papers. Southern Poverty Law Center, Montgomery, Alabama.

Interviews

Bloom, Star. Personal interview. January 22, 2010.

Cohen, Richard. Personal interview. August 4, 2009.

Eddy, Bob. Personal interview. August 21, 2009, and October 22, 2009.

Galanos, Chris. Personal interview. August 21, 2009.

Hartley, Kalliopi. Personal interview. August 26, 2009.

Kerger, Richard. Personal interview. September 3, 2009.

Riddick, Dr. LeRoy. Personal interview. August 19, 2009

Sutton, Kathy. Personal interview. August 2, 2009.

Williams, Wilbur. Personal interview. October 12, 2009, and October 17, 2009.

Court Cases/Official Documents

Beulah Mae Donald v. United Klans of America., Inc., No. 84 Civ. 0725 (S.D. Ala. 1984)

Ex Parte Josephus Anderson, 457 So. 2d 435 (Ala. Crim. App. 1984)

Ex Parte: Josephus Anderson, 457 So. 2d 446 (S.C. Ala. 1984)

Hays v. State, 518 So. 2d 749 (Ala. Crim. App. 1985)

Henry F. Hays Autopsy Report, Alabama Department of Forensic Sciences, October 6, 1997.

Josephus Anderson v. State, 542 So. 2d 292 (Ala. Crim. App. 1987)

Josephus R. Anderson v. State, 443 So. 2d 1364 (Ala. Crim. App. 1983)

Report from LeRoy Riddick, M.D., Forensic Pathologist, Department of Forensic Sciences, March 21, 1981

U.S. Cong. House Committee on the Judiciary. *Anti-Lynching Bill.* 66th Cong, 2nd Sess. H. Rept. 1027. Washington, DC: GPO, 1920.

Articles

"Appeals Court Says Donald Murderer Should Live." *New Times,* August 5, 1985. Print.

Associated Press. "Alabamian Guilty in Killing of Black." *New York Times,* May 20, 1989: 33. Print.

———. "Convict in Mobile Lynching Among Those Freed by Board." *Mobile Register,* September 11, 2000: 1A+. Print.

———. "Klan Headquarters Is Given to Black to Settle Lawsuit." *Washington Post,* May 20, 1987: A3. Print.

———. "Mob Prepares to Storm Dallas Jail for Negroes." *Tuscaloosa News,* September 4, 1933: 1. Print.

———. "Murder Trial of 2 in Klan Set." *New York Times,* February 2, 1988: A20. Print.

———. "Negro Menaced with Lynching by Gotham Mob." *Tuscaloosa News,* September 11, 1933: 1. Print.

Beidler, Philip. "Yankee Interloper and Native Son: Carl Carmer and Clarence Cason, Unlikely Twins of Alabama Exposé," *Southern Cultures,* 9.1 (2003): 18–35. Print.

"Beulah M. Donald, 67, Klan Foe." *New York Times,* September 20, 1988: D29. Print.

"Blacks Criticize Handling of Alabama Klan Case." Special to *New York Times,* June 20, 1983: B10. Print.

"Blood on the Great Seal of Alabama." *Tuscaloosa News,* originally printed in *Montgomery Advertiser,* August 15, 1933: 4. Print.

"Bloom Calls on Jewish Leaders to Curb I.L.D." *Tuscaloosa News,* August 3, 1933: 1. Print.

Boone, Buford. "KKK Mask Is Off: Klan Has Been Using County Building." *Tuscaloosa News,* May 27, 1949: 1. Print.

———. "Klan Afraid of 'Bad Man.'" *Tuscaloosa News,* May 29, 1949: 1. Print.

———. "Klan Looks Forward to Time When It Can 'Run the Town.'" *Tuscaloosa News,* May 30, 1949: 1. Print.

———. "Klansman Hits 'Dirty' Talk at KKK Meeting." *Tuscaloosa News,* May 28, 1949: 1. Print.

"Both Hit in Foot by Bullet from Gun of Officer." *Tuscaloosa News,* September 6, 1933: 1. Print.

Busby, Renee. "Cox Gets 99 Years in Prison." *Mobile Register,* June 26, 1989: 1A+. Print.

———. "Donald's Brother: Hays Must 'Deal with the Lord Now.'" *Mobile Register,* August 9, 1993: 1A+. Print.

———. "Hays House Historic?" *Mobile Register,* November 22, 1995: 1B+. Print.

———. "Hearing Held on Hays Request for New Trial, Reduced Sentence." *Mobile Register,* June 23, 1989: 1D. Print.

———. "Knowles Testifies He was Ordered to Kill." *Mobile Register,* February 5, 1987: 1A+. Print.

Busby, Renee, and Mike Casey. "Hays death sentence upheld." *Mobile Register,* August 27, 1986: 1A+. Print.

"Cabin Owner Doesn't Know if KKK Rents It." *Tuscaloosa News,* May 26, 1949: 1. Print.

"Charge to the Grand Jury." *Tuscaloosa News,* August 15, 1933: 1. Print.

"Citizens Launch Drive on Crime." *Tuscaloosa News,* October 4, 1933: 1. Print.

"Citizens Organize to Wage Crusade Against Crime Here." *Tuscaloosa News,* October 1, 1933: 1. Print.

"Citizens Praise Stand of News Against Crime." *Tuscaloosa News,* September 29, 1933: 1. Print.

"City Commission, C. of C. Directors Pledge Support in Crime Crusade." *Tuscaloosa News,* October 3, 1933: 1. Print.

"Civil Rights Investigation of Lynching Urged," *Mobile Beacon,* April 4, 1981: 1. Print.

"Clark Gives Sworn Statement Mob Had 'Drop' on Deputies." *Tuscaloosa News,* August 16, 1933: 1. Print.

"Clark Tells Miraculous Escape from Killing." *Tuscaloosa News,* August 15, 1933: 1+. Print.

Colquitt, Ron. "Expert in Evidence." *Mobile Register,* June 26, 2006: 1B+. Print.

——. "Hays Was Entitled to Military Burial Honors." *Mobile Register,* June 11, 1997: 1A+. Print.

"Court Appoints Counsel to Aid Negroes Defense." *Tuscaloosa News,* July 30, 1933: 1. Print.

"Court Clears Way to Return Former Klan Leader to Ala." *Atlanta Daily World,* May 16, 1993: 2. Print.

Drago, Arthur, Jr.. "KKK Official, Wife Charged with Fraud." *Mobile Register,* September 14, 1984: 1A+. Print.

Drago, Chip. "2 Held in '81 Murder." *Mobile Register,* June 17, 1983: 1A+. Print.

——. "Court Places Gag Order on Hays Charges." *Mobile Register,* June 18, 1983: 1A. Print.

——. "Hays Faces State Trial in Murder." *Mobile Register,* June 24, 1983: 2A. Print.

——. "Hays Out of Feds' Hands." *Mobile Register,* June 24, 1983: 1A. Print.

——. "Statement May Be Opened in Donald Slaying Case." *Mobile Register,* June 17, 1983: 1A. Print.

"Evidence Is Not Thought Enough for Indictment." *Tuscaloosa News,* October 2, 1933: 1. Print.

"Ex-Klansman Hays Gets June 6 Execution Date." *Mobile Register,* May 2, 1997: 1A+. Print.

"Ex-Klansman Sentenced to Life in Murder." *New York Times,* June 25, 1989: 18. Print.

"Face of Concern." *Birmingham News,* December 8, 1979: 2A. Print.

"Federal Grand Jury Resumes Donald Probe." *Mobile Register,* April 7, 1984: 1B. Print.

Feldman, Glenn. "Lynching in Alabama, 1889–1921." *Alabama Review,* 48.2 (1995): 114. Print.

"Fighting the I.L.D." *Tuscaloosa News,* October 8, 1933: 4. Print.

Fleeman, Michael. "Death for McVeigh." *Mobile Register,* June 14, 1997: 1A+. Print.

"Follow-up on the News; Paying Damages for a Lynching." *New York Times,* February 21, 1988: 45. Print.

Fontana, Sharron. "Let 'Yellow Mama' Rock and Roll Along." *Mobile Register,* June 10, 1997: 8A. Print.

"Guards Escort I.L.D. Lawyers out of County." *Tuscaloosa News*, August 1, 1933: 1. Print.

"Girl Thought Murdered by 'Friend.'" *Tuscaloosa News*, June 15, 1933: 1. Print.

"Grand Jury Recesses, Praises Judge Foster." *Tuscaloosa News*, September 7, 1933: 1. Print.

Hawes, Peter. "Klansmen Bloodied by Opposition in Connecticut." *Mobile Register*, March 22, 1981: 16A. Print.

"High Court Clears Way for Retrial of Two Klansmen Accused of Killing Black." *Atlanta Daily World*, January 12, 1989: 2. Print.

"I.L.D. Interference Costs State and County $1,500." *Tuscaloosa News*, August 3, 1933: 1+. Print.

"Jail Gathering Will Be Probed by Grand Jury." *Tuscaloosa News*, June 22, 1933: 1. Print.

Jennings, Tom. "3 Men Remain in Custody as Slaying Motive Sought." *Mobile Register*, March 24, 1981: 1A+. Print.

Jordan, Herb. "Hays' Hearing Postponed." *Atlanta Daily World*, May 13, 1989: 1B+. Print.

———. "Hearing Ordered on Klan Award." *Mobile Register*, February 13, 1987: 1A+. Print.

———. "Jury Rules Against Klansmen." *Mobile Register*, February 13, 1987: 1A+. Print.

Jordan, Herb and Kathy Jumper. "Figures Tells Blacks Here to Be Cool, Cautious." *Mobile Register*, March 24, 1981: 1A+. Print.

"Judge Orders Bullets to Be Taken from Body of Pippen." *Tuscaloosa News*, August 16, 1933: 1. Print.

"Judge Overrides 17-Day Recess in Lynching Inquiry." *Tuscaloosa News*, August 17, 1933: 1+. Print.

Jumper, Kathy. "Details of Killing Related by Knowles." *Mobile Register*, December 8, 1983: 1A+.

Jumper, Kathy, and Eddie Menton. "3 Charged in Donald Murder." *Mobile Register*, March 26, 1981: 1A+. Print.

———. "Hays Charged with Robbing Slaying Victim." *Mobile Register*, December 6, 1983: 1A. Print.

——. "Hays' Ex-Wife, Klansmen Testify." *Mobile Register,* December 10, 1983: 1A+. Print.

——. "Hays Family Is Bound Together by Strong Ties." *Mobile Register,* February 3, 1984: 1B. Print.

——. "Hays Found Guilty of Capital Murder." *Mobile Register,* December 11, 1983: 1A+. Print.

——. "Hays Given Death for Donald Killing." *Mobile Register,* February 2, 1984: 1A. Print.

——. "Hays Indicted for Donald Murder." *Mobile Register,* June 23, 1983: 1A+. Print.

——. "Hays Murder Trial Opening Tuesday." *Mobile Register,* December 5, 1983: 2A. Print.

——. "Hays Murder Trial Starts; Continuance Motion Denied." *Mobile Register,* December 6, 1983: 8A. Print.

——. "Hays Retrial Sought." *Mobile Register,* February 1, 1984: 1A. Print.

——. "Hays Said Looking for a Black." *Mobile Register,* December 7, 1983: 1A+. Print.

——. "Hays Sentence Delayed; Witness Sought." *Mobile Register,* February 2, 1984: 1A. Print.

——. "Hays Trial Proceedings Tense." *Mobile Register,* December 9, 1983: 1B. Print.

——. "Judge Overrules Jury, Sentences Hays to Die." *Mobile Register,* February 3, 1984: 1A. Print.

——. "Klansman Pleads Innocent to Capital Murder Charge." *Mobile Register,* July 9, 1983: 1B. Print.

——. "Mother Sought Reasons, Not Revenge, for Killing." *Mobile Register,* December 20, 1987: 1A+. Print.

——. "Police Ask for Help in Death Probe." *Mobile Register,* March 23, 1981: 1A+. Print.

——. "Rains, Hail End Fire Alert." *Mobile Register,* March 23, 1981: 1A. Print.

Jumper, Kathy, and Eddie Menton. "3 Charged in Donald Murder." *Mobile Register,* March 26, 1981: 1A+. Print.

"Jury Is Called to Begin Probe Tuesday, 9 a.m." *Tuscaloosa News,* August 14, 1933: 1+. Print.

"Jury Visits Lynching Scene." *Tuscaloosa News,* August 16, 1933: 1. Print.

Kennedy, Harold & Mark Winne. "Mayor Pledges Vigorous Drive Against Crime in Birmingham." *Birmingham News,* November 20, 1979: 1A+. Print.

"Klan Member Put to Death in Race Death." *New York Times,* June 6, 1997: A24. Print.

"Klansman Gets a Life Term." *New York Times,* April 12, 1985: A13. Print.

"Klansman Gets Life for Slaying Black." *Atlanta Daily World,* April 16, 1985: 1. Print.

"Klansman Receives Death Sentence." *Washington Post,* February 3, 1984: A20. Print.

Kornbluth, Jesse. "The Woman Who Beat the Klan." *New York Times Magazine,* November 1, 1987: 626. Print.

"The Ku Klux Klan Organized at Tuscaloosa." *West Alabama Breeze,* April 4, 1917: 6. Print.

Langford, David. "Police Doubt Hanging a Racial Incident." *Mobile Register,* March 27, 1981: 1A+. Print.

"Large Crowd Attends Donald's Funeral." *Mobile Beacon,* April 4, 1981: 1. Print.

"Local Negroes Tell I.L.D. Stay Out of Maddox Case." *Tuscaloosa News,* July 31, 1933: 1. Print.

Long, Pamela H. "Lipscomb's Plea for Hays' Life Not Unusual, Spokesman Says." *Mobile Register,* June 8, 1997: 4A. Print.

"Lynching by the Carper Baggers of 1933." *Tuscaloosa News,* August 14, 1933: 4. Print.

"Lynching Inquiry Resumed, 2-Day Session Is Likely." *Tuscaloosa News,* September 5, 1933: 1. Print.

"Maddox Murder Trials Set for Tuesday, Aug. 22." *Tuscaloosa News,* August 10, 1933: 1. Print.

"Maddox Thought Murdered by 'Friend.'" *Tuscaloosa News,* June 15, 1933: 1. Print.

"Masked Band Seizes Maddox Case Negroes." *Tuscaloosa News,* August 13, 1933: 1. Print.

McCauley, Byron. "The Consequences of Irrational Hatred." *Mobile Register,* June 7, 1997: 4A. Print.

Menton, Eddie, and Herb Jordan. "Man Found Hanged on City Street." *Mobile Register,* March 22, 1981: 1A+. Print.

"Ministers Urge All Citizens to Enlist in Crime Crusade." *Tuscaloosa News,* October 2, 1933: 1. Print.

Mitchell, Cynthia. "God Will Give the Courage." *Mobile Register,* June 24, 1989: 10B. Print.

Mitchell, Garry. "3 Charged with Murder in Hanging in Alabama." *Mobile Register,* March 26, 1981: 13A. Print.

———. "Civil Rights Leaders Hail KKK Verdict." *Mobile Register,* February 14, 1987: 1A+. Print.

———. "Imprisoned Klansman Says Slaying Ordered." *Daily Sitka Sentinel,* February 11, 1987: 7. Print.

"Mobile Murder Protested as a Lynching." *Mobile Beacon,* April 11, 1981: 1. Print.

"More Witnesses Offer Information on Shooting of Police Sgt. Ballard." *Birmingham News,* December 3, 1979: 5A. Print.

"Mystery Maze Still Unfolds Maddox Inquiry." *Tuscaloosa News,* June 18, 1933: 1. Print.

"Negro Is Lured from His Home Then Murdered." *Tuscaloosa News,* September 25, 1933: 1. Print.

"Negro Is Shot by 2 Deputies." *Tuscaloosa News,* August 14, 1933: 6. Print.

"Negro Jailed as Attack Suspect." *Tuscaloosa News,* June 16, 1933: 1. Print.

"Negro Lynched by Mississippi Gang Is Reported." *Tuscaloosa News,* July 23, 1933: 1. Print.

"Negro Retracts Previous Story in Maddox Case." *Tuscaloosa News,* June 20, 1933: 1. Print.

"Negro Says He Saw Girl Murdered." *Tuscaloosa News,* June 19, 1933: 1. Print.

"Negro Shot Three Times from Rear; Fell Under Pippen; Does Not Know Members of Mob." *Tuscaloosa News,* August 15, 1933: 1. Print.

Nelson, John. "Indiana Blasts UAB, 87–72; St. Joseph's Edges by Boston." *Birmingham News,* March 21, 1979: 1B. Print.

"No Trace Found of Third Negro." *Tuscaloosa News,* August 14, 1933: 1+.

Nolan, Ben. "Tulsa Kills Jag Hopes, 69–68." *Mobile Register,* March 21, 1981: 1B. Print.

Pienciak, Richard. "Caller Claims He Killed Four." *Mobile Register,* March 20, 1981: 1A+. Print.

"Pippen Murder Trial Continues." *Tuscaloosa News,* August 1, 1933: 1. Print.

"The Press: Mr. Graves Takes a Walk." *Time,* March 4, 1946. Print.

"Races: Lynchings Nos. 10 & 11." *Time,* August 18, 1930. Print.

"Radicals Intent on Interfering in Maddox Case." *Tuscaloosa News,* August 7, 1933: 1. Print.

Reeks, Anne. "$250,000 Bonds Are Set in Mobile Hanging Case." *Mobile Register,* March 27, 1981: 1+. Print.

———. "Alleged Perjurer in Donald Case Held." *Mobile Register,* June 13, 1981: 2B. Print.

———. "Bail for 3 Men Accused in Donald Case Reduced." *Mobile Register,* May 9, 1981: 1A+. Print.

———. "Bail Set for Men Charged in Donald Slaying." *Mobile Register,* March 28, 1981: 1. Print.

———. "Donald Probe Renewed; All 3 Suspects Freed." *Mobile Register,* June 6, 1981: 1A. Print.

———. "Expert Links Bullet to Anderson's Gun." *Mobile Register,* March 20, 1981: 1B. Print.

"Reward of $400 Posted by State in Cross Death." *Tuscaloosa News,* September 27, 1933: 1. Print.

"Robert Shelton, 73, Leader of Big Klan Faction." *New York Times,* March 20, 2003: B8. Print.

Schmidt, William. "Black Lawyer Pressing Klan Appeal for Parade." *New York Times,* December 24, 1983: 8. Print.

"SCLC Says It Has Name of Witness." *Birmingham News,* December 2, 1979: 5A. Print.

Scroggs, William. "Mob Violence: An Enemy of Both Races." Southern Sociological Conference. New Orleans. April 19, 1916. Address. W. S. Hoole Special Collections Library, The University of Alabama, Tuscaloosa.

"Shall We Accept the Challenge?" *Tuscaloosa News,* September 27, 1933: 1. Print.

Sloan, Ross. "In an Execution's Aftermath, Let Us Kill Capital Punishment." *Mobile Register,* June 9, 1997: 6A. Print.

Smith, Buddy. "Nature Factor in Eliminating Obscure Legend from Baldwin." *Mobile Register,* March 22, 1981: 4B. Print.

"Society Holds No Place for the Klan." *Mobile Register,* February 14, 1987: 4A. Print.

"Sound Off." *Mobile Register,* June 6, 1997: 2A. Print.

Stolberg, Sheryl Gay. "Senate Issues Apology over Failure on Lynching Law." *New York Times,* June 14, 2005: A15. Print.

"Sunrise." *Mobile Register,* March 21, 1981: 2A. Print.

Taylor, Nadia M. "Street Renamed for Michael Donald." *Mobile Register,* May 17, 2006: 1B. Print.

Taylor, Sandra Baxley. "Anderson Jury Apparently Stood 10-2 for Acquittal." *Birmingham News,* March 21, 1981: 1A+. Print.

"Three Arrested for Activity in Jail Gathering." *Tuscaloosa News,* June 28, 1933: 1. Print.

Toner, Robin. "A Mother's Struggle with the Klan." Special to *New York Times,* March 8, 1987. Print.

"US Reopens Hangman Killing." *Mobile Register,* May 26, 1983: 1B. Print.

Van Hoose, Alf. "Top Plow-Hand Shealy Cuts Tiger Furrow; Lifts No. 1 Bama out of a Deep Hole 25–18." *Birmingham News,* December 2, 1979: 1C+. Print.

Waldrep, Christopher. "War of Words: The Controversy over the Definition of Lynching, 1899–1940." *Journal of Southern History,* 6.1 (2000): 75–100. Print.

"Weather Forecast Favorable." *Birmingham News,* March 21, 1979: 1A. Print.

"White Bandits Force Negro on Long Night Ride." *Tuscaloosa News,* July 10, 1933: 3. Print.

Wilson, Austin. "LSU Powers by Hogs, 72–56." *Birmingham News,* March 21, 1979: 1B. Print.

Wilson, Michael. "Bennie Jack's Klan." *Mobile Register,* June 3, 1997: 1A+. Print.

———. "Cases Closed." *Mobile Register,* June 4, 1997: 1A+. Print.

———. "Family Members Plead for Henry Hays' Life," *Mobile Register,* June 4, 1997: 15A. Print.

———. "The Final Hours." *Mobile Register,* June 5, 1997: 1A+. Print.

———. "Hays Made Confession to Minister." *Mobile Register,* June 8, 1997: 1A+. Print.

———. "Hays Put to Death." *Mobile Register,* June 7, 1997: 1A+. Print.

———. "Jury's $7 Million Verdict Mostly a Paper Victory." *Mobile Register,* June 4, 1997: 14A. Print.

———. "Klansman's Death Row Appeal Rejected by Circuit Court." *Mobile Register,* June 8, 1996: 2B. Print.

———. "Michael Didn't Come Home." *Mobile Register,* June 1, 1997: 1A+. Print.

———. "Mock Hanging by Police Caused Furor 5 Years Before." *Mobile Register,* June 1, 1997: 18A. Print.

———. "New Trial for Hays Denied." *Mobile Register,* March 7, 1995: 1B+. Print.

———. "Old Friend Offers Surprise Alibi for Henry Hays." *Mobile Register,* June 4, 1997: 15A. Print.

———. "Raised in Hate." *Mobile Register,* June 2, 1997: 1A+. Print.

———. "Warden Questions Minister's Version." *Mobile Register,* June 13, 1997: 1A+. Print.

———. "Witness to an Execution." *Mobile Register,* June 10, 1997: 1A+. Print.

Winne, Mark. "Ballard's Accused Slayer Glares as Warrants Served at Hospital." *Birmingham News,* December 8, 1979: 2A. Print.

———. "Chief Retires Ballard Car in His Honor." *Birmingham News,* December 5, 1979: 5A. Print.

———. "Police Work in Sorrow on Ballard Case." *Birmingham News,* December 1, 1979: 2A. Print.

———. "Slain Officer: 'Good, Gentle . . . Christian.'" *Birmingham News,* November 30, 1979: 1A+. Print.

———. "Suspect in Policeman Murder Has Arrest Record Covering Almost All His Adult Life." *Birmingham News,* December 6, 1979: 1A+. Print.

———. "'Unity May Be Sergeant's Legacy.'" *Birmingham News,* December 4, 1979: 1A+. Print.

Winne, Mark, and Andrew Kilpatrick. "'Oh God, I Need Help,' Dying Officer Radios." *Birmingham News,* November 20, 1979: 1A+. Print.

"Wounded Negro Appears Before the Grand Jury." *Tuscaloosa News,* August 15, 1933: 1. Print.

"Youth of 20 Who Lives Near the Crime, Taken." *Tuscaloosa News,* June 16, 1933: 1. Print.

Books

Allen, James, Hilton Als, John Lewis, and Leon Litwack. *Without Sanctuary: Lynching Photography in America.* Santa Fe: Twin Palms Publishers, 2000. Print.

Apel, Dora, and Shawn Michelle Smith. *Lynching Photographs.* Berkeley: The University of California Press, 2007. Print.

Branch, Taylor. *Parting the Waters.* New York: Touchstone, 1988. Print.

———. *Pillar of Fire.* New York: Simon & Schuster Paperbacks, 1998. Print.

Brundage, W. Fitzhugh. *The Southern Past: A Clash of Race and Memory.* Cambridge: The Belknap Press of Harvard University Press, 2005. Print.

Carmer, Carl. *Stars Fell on Alabama.* Tuscaloosa: The University of Alabama Press, 1990. Print.

Carr, Cynthia. *Our Town.* New York: Crown Publishers, 2006. Print.

Cash, W. J. *The Mind of the South.* New York: Vintage Books, 1941. Print.

Cason, Clarence. *90° in the Shade.* Tuscaloosa: The University of Alabama Press, 2001. Print.

Chadbourn, James Harmon. *Lynching and the Law.* Chapel Hill: The University of North Carolina Press, 1933. Print.

Dees, Morris, and Steve Fiffer. *A Season for Justice: The Life and Times of Civil Rights Lawyer Morris Dees.* New York: Charles Scribner's Sons, 1991. Print.

Delaney, Caldwell. *The Story of Mobile.* Mobile: Gill Press, 1962. Print.

Dray, Philip. *At the Hands of Persons Unknown: The Lynching of Black America.* New York: Random House, 2002. Print.

Feldman, Glenn. *Politics, Society, and the Klan in Alabama 1915–1949.* Tuscaloosa: The University of Alabama Press, 1999. Print.

Hall, Jacquelyn David. *Revolt Against Chivalry: Jessie Daniel Ames and the Women's Campaign Against Lynching.* New York: Columbia University Press, 1993. Print.

Hall, Nathan. *Hate Crime.* Portland: Willan Publishing, 2005. Print.

Hechler, Ken. *Working with Truman: A Personal Memoir of the White House Years.* Columbia: University of Missouri Press, 1982. Print.

Ifill, Sherrilyn. *On the Courthouse Lawn: Confronting the Legacy of Lynching.* Boston: Beacon Press, 2007. Print.

Kelley, Robin. *Hammer and Hoe: Alabama Communists During the Great Depression.* Chapel Hill: The University of North Carolina Press, 1990. Print.

Madison, James. *A Lynching in the Heartland.* New York: Palgrave, 2001. Print.

Margolick, David. *Strange Fruit: Billie Holiday, Cafe Society, and an Early Cry for Civil Rights.* Philadelphia: Running Press, 2000. 25–29. Print.

Markovitz, Jonathan. *Legacies of Lynching: Racial Violence and Memory.* Minneapolis: University of Minnesota Press, 2004. Print.

McWhorter, Diane. *Carry Me Home*. New York: Touchstone, 2001. Print.

Milton, George Fort. *Lynchings and What They Mean: General Findings of the Southern Commission on the Study of Lynching*. Atlanta: The Commission, 1931. Print. Courtesy of W. S. Hoole Special Collections Library, The University of Alabama, Tuscaloosa.

———. *The Plight of Tuscaloosa: Mob Murders, Community Hysteria, Official Incompetence*. Atlanta: Southern Commission on the Study of Lynching. Print. Courtesy of W. S. Hoole Special Collections Library, The University of Alabama, Tuscaloosa.

Newton, Michael. *The Ku Klux Klan*. Jefferson, North Carolina: McFarland & Company, 2007. Print.

Pfeifer, Michael. *Rough Justice: Lynching and American Society, 1974–1947*. Urbana, IL: University of Illinois Press, 2004. Print.

Raper, Arthur. *The Tragedy of Lynching*. New York: Dover Publications, Inc, 2003. Print.

Roberts, Gene & Hank Klibanoff. *The Race Beat: The Press, the Civil Rights Struggle, and the Awakening of a Nation*. New York: Vintage Books, 2006. Print.

Sellers, James B. *History of the University of Alabama Volume One: 1818–1902*. Tuscaloosa: The University of Alabama Press, 1953. Print.

Shay, Frank. *Judge Lynch*. New York: Ives Washburn, Inc., 1938. Print.

Till-Mobley, Mamie, and Christopher Benson. *Death of Innocence: The Story of the Hate Crime that Changed America*. New York: Random House, 2003. Print.

Tolnay, Stewart, and E. M. Beck. *A Festival of Violence: An Analysis of Southern Lynchings, 1882–1930*. Urbana, Illinois: The University of Illinois Press, 1995. Print.

Waldrep, Christopher. *African Americans Confront Lynching*. New York: Rowman & Littlefield Publishers, Inc., 2009. Print.

———. *Lynching in America: A History in Documents*. New York: New York University Press, 2006. Print.

———. *The Many Faces of Judge Lynch: Extralegal Violence and Punishment in America*. New York: Palgrave Macmillan, 2002. Print.

Ward, Gladys. *Life of Ryland Randolph*. Thesis. Tuscaloosa: The University of Alabama, 1932. Print.

Wells, Ida B. *On Lynching.* New York: Humanity Books, 2002. Print.

———. "A Red Record." In *Southern Horrors and Other Writings: The Anti-Lynching Campaign of Ida B. Wells, 1892–1900.* Ed. Jacqueline Jones Royster. Boston: Bedford Books, 1997. Print.

Wexler, Laura. *Fire in a Canebrake: The Last Mass Lynching in America.* New York: Charles Scribner's Sons, 2003. Print.

White, Walter. *Rope and Faggot.* Notre Dame, Indiana: University of Notre Dame Press, 2001. Print.

Williamson, Joel. *A Rage for Order: Black-White Relations in the American South Since Emancipation.* New York: Oxford University Press, 1986. Print.

Wyatt-Brown, Bertram. *The Shaping of Southern Culture: Honor, Grace, and War, 1760s–1880s.* Chapel Hill: The University of North Carolina Press, 2001. Print.

———. *Southern Honor: Ethics and Behavior in the Old South.* New York: Oxford University Press, 1982. Print.

Electronic Texts

"Hearing on the Senate Judiciary Committee on the Nomination of Clarence Thomas to the Supreme Court." Electronic Text Center, University of Virginia Library. October 11, 1991. Etext.lib.virginia.edu. Web. July 8, 2010. <http://etext.lib.virginia.edu/etcbin/toccer-new-yitna?id=UsaThom&images=images/modeng&data=/lv6/workspace/yitna&tag=public&part=24>.

King, Martin Luther. "Letter from a Birmingham Jail." African Studies Center. University of Pennsylvania. Web. July 22, 2010. <http://www.africa.upenn.edu/Articles_Gen/Letter_Birmingham.html>.

NAACP. "NAACP History: Anti-lynching Bill." Web. July 31, 2010. <http://www.naacp.org/pages/naacp-history-anti-lynching-bill>.

Peter, Paul. *8 Who Lie in the Death House.* NP: National Committee for the Defense of Political Prisoners, 1933. Web. August 1, 2010. <archive.lib.msu.edu/DMC/AmRad/eightwholie.pdf>.

"Remarks by the President at Reception Commemorating the Enactment of the Matthew Shepherd and James Byrd, Jr. Hate Crimes Prevention Act." White House, Washington D.C. October 28, 2009. Whitehouse.gov. Web.

June 28, 2010. <http://www.whitehouse.gov/the-press-office/remarks-president-reception-commemorating-enactment-matthew-shepard-and-james-byrd->.

Woodham, Rebecca. "Buford Boone." September 24, 2008. *Encyclopedia of Alabama.* Web. July 8, 2010. <http://www.encyclopediaofalabama.org/face/Article.jsp?id=h-1783>.

Radio

"Interview with Robert Shelton." By Marsha Tompkins. WBAI, New York. December 24, 1969. Web. August 1, 2010.<http://newstalgia.crooksandliars.com/gordonskene/all-hate-all-time-conversation-robert>.

Television

KKK: Inside American Terror. By Mike Sinclair, Nan Byrne, and Daniele Anastasion. National Geographic Channel. October 15, 2008. Television.

The Last Lynching. Discovery Channel. October 13, 2008. Television.

INDEX